JUST A FEW GOOD MEN

7 Strategies to Jump Start Your Men's Ministry

A Spiritual Guide

Foreword By
Rev. Frank D. Tucker, Pastor

Tillman, Jr., Allen L.
    "Just A Few Good Men" / by Allen L. Tillman, Jr.

ISBN-13: 978-1-4276-2313-3

Scripture references in this book are from the King James
Version of the Holy Bible (unless otherwise noted).

Empowerment Consulting Group Publications
P.O. Box 7516
Langley Park, Maryland 20787
R2Recovery@aol.com
www.roadtorecovery.org

Allen L. Tillman, Jr.'s books are available
for special promotions and seminars.
For details please contact us at the above noted address.

First Edition©2007

Printed in the United States by Morris Publishing
3212 East Highway 30
Kearney, NE 68847
1-800-650-7888

In loving memory of

Claudia Ford

and

Emma Williams

TABLE OF CONTENTS

ACKNOWLEDGEMENTS

To my Lord and Savior, Jesus the Anointed One, who took a filthy rag and used it to knock the dust off some ministries, so He may be glorified and the Kingdom become on earth as it is in heaven.

I must thank my wife, Sarah, for her love and sweet benevolent heart that allowed me to often spend money that many times disturbed our budget. My wife, almost single handedly, put together first class programs for every ministry event God allowed us to sponsor. When others were laughing and murmuring, she was always optimistic and prayerful. *"An excellent wife is the crown of her husband."* *(Proverbs 12:4)*

I am indebted to many individuals both living and those who have gone home to be with the Lord. It is with the utmost respect and sincere appreciation that I recognize those who offered invaluable time to share their thoughts, those who offered their respected talents and those who contributed to this vision. Hail to the warriors of worship who are determined to shape a new frontier in men's ministries. A great example is King David who sought to prepare a blueprint for a temple, but God prohibited King

David from building that Temple *(I Chronicles 22:8 – "But the word of the Lord came to me, saying, 'You have shed much blood and have made great wars: you shall not build a house, for my name, because you have shed much blood on the earth in my sight.'")*. He realized that a vision of such magnitude would be a collective one. I Chronicles 23:1-5 states, *"And he gathered together all the leaders of Israel, with priests and the Levites. Now, the Levites were numbered from the age of thirty years and above; and the number of males was thirty-eight thousand. 'Of these twenty-four thousand were to look after the work of the house of the Lord, six thousand were officers and judges, four thousand were gatekeepers, and four thousand praised the Lord, with musical instruments, which I made,' said David, for giving praise."* This scripture further echoes the sentiment that God does not intend for one man to institute this type of vision.

To the evolution of the church from the traditional to the "out of the box" ministry experimentations, I am thankful to God for the great local and national leaders who put aside denominations and personal agendas for the benefit of a more unified men's church community. When no one else believed in the vision, these men listened to God. Because of their sincere desire to unify men of Christ in the

21st Century, these men postponed engagements, probably with gratuitous opportunities, and shared their gifts without hesitation. I am humbled to mention such legendary names as Reverend Daniel Mangrum, Bishop Alfred Owens, Reverend Frank Tucker, Reverend Freddie Davis, Reverend Harold Lewis, Reverend Stephen Tucker, Reverend Matthew Watley, Reverend Don Melvin and Reverend Eldridge Spearman.

Lifetime committed advocates for men's ministries in the Body of Christ such as Deacon Terry Proctor, Minister Don Hunter, Deacon Gregory Wheeler, Deacon Roy Few, Trustee John Lanier, Oscar Watson, Deacon Kevin Johnson, Paul Shively, Deacon Sylvester McCoy, Minister George Bartley, Don Habersham, Pastor Anthony Minter, Maestro Irvin Royster, Ed Miller, Minister Albert Farmer, Vernoy Hite, Kenneth Mitchell, Jerome Austin, Orlonzo Chappell, Dr. Llewellyn Felton, Minister Raimon Nelson, Deacon Parrish Rembert, Sr., Deacon Fred Williams, Deacon Kenneth Swift, Minister Cleveland Bates, Rev. Michael Nettles, Deacon Lamar Pearson, Edward Tellis, and many others – may heaven shine on you.

I would also like to salute the institutions that vow to carry out the mandate to bring men back into the fold like Cornerstone Bible Baptist Church, First Baptist Church of Randolph Street

NW, First Baptist Church of Minnesota Avenue, Good Success Christian Church, Lincoln Park United Methodist, Pilgrim Rest Baptist Church, New Commandment Baptist Church, Reid Temple A.M.E., and Greater Mount Calvary Holy Church.

This undertaking would not have been possible without the generosity or understanding the significance of men taking their rightful place by these bold and beautiful women of God. Beginning with my mother, Edith Cline Tillman, much like the mother of Jesus, she stays on the frontline. I am reminded of the vote of confidence given to Timothy claiming, **"when I call to remembrance the genuine faith that is in you which dwelt first in your grandmother and your mother Eunice, and I am persuaded is in you also."** (II Timothy 1:5-6) If there is a strand of decency in my spiritual DNA, it is because of my mother and my Aunt Clara Simpson (who stood in for my grandmother).

The Apostle Paul realized the significance of both men and women stating, **"Greet Priscilla and Aquila and the household of Onesiphorus. Erastus stayed in Corinth, but Trophimus I have left in Miletus sick. Eubulus greets you as well as Pudens, Linus, Claudia, and all the brethren."** (II Timothy 4:19-21) I must also celebrate those women who sowed in the ministry of men such as Deaconess

Martha Bratcher, Gwendolyn Miller, Deaconess Elsie Brown, Sylvia Kinard, Deaconess Mildred Jean Toliver, Reverend Joyce Brooks, Deaconess Carsino Johnson, Deaconess Easter Harris, Mother Mildred Dryden, Reverend Catherine Bego, Denise Hunter, Deaconess Naomi Rembert, Minister Miriam Suggs, Deaconess Mazy Slade, Kimberly Nelson, Deaconess Dorothy Baynes and Deaconess Barbara Watson-Mickens.

I am of the mindset that *"Maturity of a plant is contingent upon the maturity of the soil."* In other words, the plant grows based on how seasoned the soil that undergirds it. I have been blessed that these mature men allowed me to grow under their guidance - - in the persons of Deacon Percy Baynes and Trustee William Slade. Psalms 1 contends, **"Blessed is the man who walks not in the counsel of the ungodly, nor stands in the path of sinners."** I believe every Timothy needs a Paul to walk with him. Thank you, gentlemen for taking a gamble on an unsure bet.

To the treatment facilities who put aside their various modalities and took a chance by allowing us to assume the responsibility of their clients in a desperate effort to expose them to the spiritual love and healing power of Jesus Christ. This list includes: LaCasa Shelter, Teen Challenge, Blair Shelter, Gospel Rescue

Ministries, Father Hines' Soup Kitchen, Third Street Church of God, and Central Union Mission.

To my brothers (Jerome, Kevin, Bryan, Courtney, and Maulana), my sisters (Sharon and Brenda), my children (Annette, Brooke, and Allen III), my grandchildren (Darnell, Dylan, Darrin, and Blair), in-laws (Cassandra, Mashelle, Nicole, Chryl, Maudisa, DoWaine, and Warren), aunts, uncles, cousins, nieces, nephews, and the family leaders Shirley Hall, George Tillman, Constance Hines, Lemmuel Cline, Betty Sedgwick, and Gus Tillman. A very special acknowledgement to my dad, Allen L. Tillman, Sr., who instilled his many gifts and determination in me which sustains me through life. *"I love you Dad, save me a seat in heaven."*

To every evangelist, preacher, teacher, and layperson, *keep your hand in the hand of Our Savior.* To every man in America who cannot rest until the men of God return to the place of God. Hold your head up and listen to God. And last, but certainly not least, my editor, Rita Thompson-Joyner, of *Oh, For Joy! Enterprises,* whom God placed in my life for such a time as this.

Be Blessed,
Allen

FOREWORD

JUST A FEW GOOD MEN is a product of the spiritual passion, spiritual struggle, and the creative vision of a man committed to serve God by challenging men to discover a full relationship with their Creator. Minister Tillman's personal experience with deliverance motivates a relentless passion to expose every man to that power which affirms his wholeness. The authentic claim of the Divine in one's life is expressed in the determination to minister in obedience to God.

Minister Tillman's guide to men's ministry grows out of the spiritual and practical struggle to put into action what his heart and passion desired and God demanded. The process of developing a men's ministry is not a simple task, however, it is a most important undertaking for Christian ministry. Minister Tillman offers clear and direct steps for those persons seriously interested in the task of growing a men's ministry. The suggestions offered come out of a commitment to reach and inspire men to participate in a process of helping others to grow into a healthy relationship with Christ.

Minister Tillman helps us understand that men's ministry development requires a passion that has its origin in a call of God, as well as, a vision and mission based on the word of God, a commitment drawn from a relationship with Christ, and a persistence that is grounded in a willingness to accept the cross.

I encourage all men who want to grow men's ministries to draw upon the fruit produced by the practical experiences recorded in the following pages. The suggestions will be important information to enhance your efforts, avoid some pitfalls, and lead to potential success.

Minister Tillman again has produced another testimony to his love, passion, and commitment to reach all men for a forgiving God. We are blessed to have this zeal for building men into the wholeness expected by the Creator.

Reverend Frank D. Tucker, Pastor
First Baptist Church
Randolph Street, NW
Washington, DC

INTRODUCTION

Tell me not, in mournful numbers
"Life is but an empty dream!"
For the soul is dead that slumbers,
And things are not what they seem.
Henry Wadsworth Longfellow

From the Internet, magazines, cable television, pornography, videos, DVDs, to being on the down low - this is probably the most difficult period in history to be a man of God. This challenge was never more evident than when it was demonstrated by a group of young student athletes, with the authorization of the coach at a major university (which will remain nameless), hired female strippers to berate and disgrace themselves to celebrate their victory in a lacrosse championship game. Most men feel as long as they can keep up productivity, leadership, and financial responsibility, their attempt at a spiritual relationship is encouraged, not mandated. Weak character is defined by those who have fallen to what Malcolm X categorized as the destructive ills of our society "cigarettes, alcohol, and drugs". Strong character is defined by those who conquer "by any means necessary". Yet, the strongest attribute a man can have is the character of Jesus Christ.

There are two words that are commonly used to represent the state or condition of humanity (the human race) or human beings. Those words are "man" and "mankind". Webster's New World Dictionary of the American Language College Edition defines man as "a combining form meaning man or person; specifically a member of a (specified) nation." Of all the things God created, man was His greatest masterpiece. Man is the only thing that God created in His own image like a proud father and His son. Genesis 1:26 states, **"And God said, 'Let us make man in our own image.'"** God breathed life into man. Unlike any of His other creations, God gave man an intellect. He gave man a moral nature, communication skills, and His Spirit. Nothing else was designed after God, for woman was fashioned from the rib of man.

There are 98 million men in America 18 years of age and older.[1] Obviously, man was terribly significant to God. He made more of man than He did anything else. God gave man dominion over everything in the earth. God gave man a moral obligation to the world. Yet, as we look at the nation's moral fabric unravel, because of man's pursuit of pleasure at any expense, one can only ponder, that this could not have been God's intention for man. When

---

[1]   Morley, Patrick, *"A Look in the Mirror – An Equipping Newsletter for Men – The State of Men in America: Foundation for the Battle for Men's Souls,"* Number 88, 2001.

asked about morality, Greek philosopher Socrates said, *"We are discussing no small matter, but how we ought to live."*[2] We have witnessed the standard of living drop like the temperature in Alaska on a January morning. From terrorism to euthanasia, man has taken complete advantage of the freewill God has given him, creating a society that seems to be governed by psychological egoism.

Man has to accept the responsibility for the condition of the world. In our attempt to achieve the American dream for ourselves and our families, we have been left unfulfilled and worse, we are on our way to hell. By worldly standards, man's rationale is justified. Less than 35% of men in America live by biblical principles.[3] But, who is the twenty-first century man?

Is the image of manhood this shadowy, multifaceted, utilitarian figure that will ultimately devour creation? Or is he just the victim of an evolutionary society? Perhaps, through the dispensation of grace, God is giving man an opportunity to redeem himself; and that can only be accomplished by first taking our rightful place with God.

---

2   Mannion, James, *"The Everything Philosophy Book"*, 2002.
3   Morley, Patrick, *"A Look in the Mirror – An Equipping Newsletter for Men – The State of Men in America: Foundation for the Battle for Men's Souls"*, Number 88, 2001.

Since man was created by God and for God, we ought to embrace a commitment to please Him. More often than not, men feel that if we simply ignore this responsibility, we have a license to live as we please. We then waste a lot of what God has given us, while we pursue temporal things. It all starts with the fellowship of Jesus Christ. The world won't come together until men and the church come together. There are indications that despite the condition of the world, men want to do what is morally and ethically best for society.

The average brain contains twelve billion cells. It has been said that the average person only uses 10% of those cells over a lifetime. Of that 10%, very little is used to nurture our spiritual development. We are taught to use them to acquire the things in life. We are taught to maximize two freedoms – the right to love and the right to work.

Although, we have all been born with spiritual gifts to be used for the glory of God, God also wants us to use our physical gifts to His glory as well. First, however, there must be a transformation of the mind.

Modern psychology, twelve-step programs and other valiant modalities have been created to have a positive influence on the character of men. They have exhausted every approach to avoid dependence on biblical principles to rebuild man's character. Psychosocial theorists, such as Erik Erikson, view religious ideologies as merely an influence in our societal systems.[4] They believe that following biblical principles has little or no impact on our biological and psychological systems. Yet, the bible clearly declares that all things work through the Spirit of God.

Students of psychology argue the Word of God has a limited impact on a man's physical and psyche. For example, Greek philosopher Aristotle was a proponent of moral virtue, which contends that character traits being fundamental and that the right actions are those that result from good character; however, if an individual's behavior is not patterned after the image of Jesus Christ it is unlikely that he will demonstrate good character.

Most men have good intentions, but the road to hell is paved with good intentions. There is a huge distinction between having good intentions and living a godly life. In Matthew, Chapter 7, Jesus reminds us, *"... wide is the gate and broad is the way that leads to destruction and there are many who go in by it."*

---

[4]   Mannion, James *"The Everything Philosophy Book"*, 2002.

This book is written to offer inspiration and guidance for building and rebuilding men's ministries in a way that will compel men to come, nurture their spirits, and equip them to reach their God-given destiny. This book seeks to heighten awareness within the Body of Christ as to why men are turned off by church. Men need to be taught how we can biblically address the spiritual causes of our social, economic, environmental, and political concerns. The church must present forums that allow men to deal with and embrace the relationship between God and man's dominion.

Our challenge, as twenty-first century men, is to acknowledge the responsibility God has given us. We must lean wholly on Him to help us begin to live more godly lives. It is the only way we can reach the extraordinary destines He has ordained for us. After all, we are His most magnificent creation.

PASSION
"FROM DESPERATION TO INSPIRATION"

PASSION DEVOTIONAL
(Pray This Prayer Before You Read The Next Chapter)

Heavenly Father, Oh how I bless Thee
Oh, how I love thee
My Father thank You for being my God
Thank You for Your divine assignment
Lord, I know I do not deserve Your affection
It is only by Your grace I have known thee
Blessed by Your name

God, I pray that this passion You
have imparted in me will glorify Your name
Let me first be passionate for Thee
and I know then I can be passionate
for this ministry

Touch my mind that I may make decisions
built up in Your wisdom

Let Thy will be done and not mine
God let me not get upset with those
You have not touched
I accept the burden given to me
Stay nigh to Thee as I walk in uncharted territory

Let me demonstrate Your love to those who
oppose Your vision
Glory to God in the highest
Praise Him forever and ever

AMEN

8

PASSION
"FROM DESPERATION TO INSPIRATION"

"We must accept the responsibility that God has put upon us, not only to be good husbands and fathers and builders of our community, but God is now calling upon the despised and the rejected to become the cornerstone and the builders of a new world."
--Minister Louis Farrakhan at the Million Man March
Washington, DC - October 17, 1995

Any successful ministry must be driven and sustained by passion. Passion is the key to an effective ministry. Most men think of the word passion as relating to something feminine. After all – perfumes and various feminine products are named after it. My dentist is David Scott, DDS. He is perhaps one of the country's better dentists. He is the most passionate man I have ever met when it comes to his profession. He represents all the attributes of passion. First, he loves what he does, as if he were born to do it. Staying in the forefront of education is his second passion. A passionate man has to keep up to date with the changes in ministry. Just like a doctor. Would you want a doctor who continues to use the same old techniques even though technology is advancing? Outdated methods consume time and are often inaccurate. Accuracy requires steadfast advancement in the industry of your passion.

9

To be passionate and uninformed merely frustrates and may even crush the desire of the individual. Passionate individuals are usually experts in their passion. They are tireless workers. They are so absorbed that they look for every opportunity to host or attend forums and events that celebrate and recognize their passion. They are generally the leader or at least among the leadership. The Apostle Paul also defines passion. Whether on the right side or the wrong side, he was very passionate. The first century Christian's world was forever changed because of Paul's passion. I would go as far as saying that passion may be a condition for greatness. Whatever Paul embarked upon, whether it was persecution or evangelism, his unbridled passion led him to a leadership position.

John Maxwell contends in his *"Maxwell Leadership Bible, Lessons in Leadership from the Word of God"*, you have to run with passion and it translates into purpose and perspective. Hebrews 12:1-3 states that ***"Therefore we also, since we are surrounded by so great a cloud of witnesses, let us lay aside every weight and the sin which so easily ensnares us and let us run with endurance the race that is set before us looking unto Jesus, the author and finisher of our faith, who for the joy that was set before Him endured the cross, despising the shame, and has set down at*** *the right hand of the throne of God.***"** In other words, I believe passion has momentum that must be capitalized upon. As in sports, when you have the momentum you do not stop until the momentum has been quenched. Old "mo" (meaning momentum) can carry you beyond your normal endurance both physically and mentally.

The Apostle Paul was an expert at taking momentum and running with it. I believe this is what he was attempting to translate to the congregation at Corinth. He suspected that the environment at Corinth was not conducive to the church. This city of Corinth was the chief city in Greece. Its location situated upon two harbors was at the crossroads for travelers and traders and visitors from Italy, Spain, Asia Minor, Phoenicia and Egypt. This city was dominated by the Pagan religious practices and spiritual influence of Aphrodite and Ascleplus. Corinth was a city full of immorality and once had 1,000 sacred prostitutes that were leaders or servants to the temple "The Temple of Aphrodite."

While others cannot totally embrace another's passion, the passion for the ministry can. Paul wrote many letters to the Corinthians desperately trying to pontificate the necessity of remaining focused despite the dominating immoral environment in Greece. Passion becomes advantageous when negative spirits encompass the ministry. The ministry will be sustained in any environment if passion is at the core of the ministry. Since passion is an anointed spirit from God, it is God's gift to the designated one. Moses, Joshua, Samuel, Gideon, Abraham, Jacob and Isaac had it. Each one of the biblical giants suffered greatly because of their passion. When their passion was misdirected to cause great harm to them and others, it was because the passion is still powerful no matter how we use it. That is why we should allow God to direct our passion. Perhaps, this is why the bible says, ***"Trust in the Lord (or trust Him with your passion) with all your heart. In all thy ways acknowledge Him and He shall direct (the passion) your path."*** *(Proverbs 3:5-6)*

Your passion will upset and expose other leaders of the ministry that lack passion. Yet, if you hold out those who oppose you will ultimately become curious to your effort and embrace your passion. Just like Nicodemus and Jesus. Nicodemus was connected to a sect that admittedly opposed Jesus. Nevertheless, Jesus' passion caused Nicodemus to investigate the ministry of Jesus. Their encounter led Jesus to share the formula for His passion. Jesus informed Nicodemus that he must be born again. That is how passion transfers. You need a rebirth from the Holy Spirit to be anointed with the passion needed for God's vision. Even though God anoints you with passion, you are still responsible for focusing and maintaining your gift. Case in point, Sampson had the passion to lead, but it was misdirected because he took it for granted. Sampson never nurtured his gift. A gift from God such as passion when nurtured will blossom and develop to be more powerful than its original state.

Generally, our passion initially pursues us from the onset. Passion is like the fire shut up in your bones. (*Jeremiah 20:9*) No matter where you run or where you hide, you will never escape yours. It will come in your dreams and chase you in your nightmares. A clear indication of how great one's passion is would be to realize you would actually, serve for free, you would even invest money in it. I believe every human being has a passion within. Perhaps, the key indicator of passion is, if in fact, in order for the passion to come into fruition you do not have to be in charge. One definition states that passion is the *"the object of such enthusiasm"*.[5] It is also defined as *"The sufferings of Christ in the period following the last supper and including the crucifixion"*. These definitions tell me that passion is no small emotion. Martin Luther King's sermon entitled *"The Drum Major's Instinct"* eloquently expresses how passion will

---

[5] *Webster's II New College Dictionary*, Houghton Mifflin Company, 1999.

allow you to sacrifice your personal agenda in order to make your passion a reality.

Passion is like an invisible fuel and without it destiny is delayed. Case in point, several years ago, I participated in a Men's Day Program at one of the local churches. The Men's Day Program is an event that is traditionally provided by Baptist churches to feature the men of the church and to attract potential male members. During this blessed event, one can anticipate seeing more men in the church. This is the one service of the year when men feel obligated to be in attendance (which is very rare). It is often a very stimulating and moving experience. It is not a coincidence that more men join the church at this event than at any other. It is one of the few opportunities where men of faith get to make a statement to the rest of the world, demonstrate his faith and appeal to the unsaved man. In other words, the men of the church pull out the fireworks. The Sunday program is usually preceded by a Saturday prayer breakfast and several other male-oriented activities a week (or month) leading up to the Men's Day program. In spite of all of the hoopla, it is still a challenge to get men to recognize this event and participate in it.

In an effort to overcome the lack of men in our churches, a group of local churches committed over the years to combine each choirs for our respective Men's Day programs.

Ephesians 4:3-4 says, *"Endeavoring to keep the unity of the Spirit in the bond of peace. There is one body and one Spirit, even as ye were called in one hope of your calling."* Despite our denominational differences, it was more important to unite in Spirit. Even with collaborative efforts, the attendance of the men for the program that year wasn't very encouraging. As a matter of fact, that particular year, it was the worst ever. The church was filled with women. There were more men in the choir than in the congregation. It was as if a dark spirit hovered over the sanctuary. I began to ask the Lord, "What is going on?" I imagined how discouraging it must be for a man who is new in Christ to witness this spectacle.

On a day to celebrate, with all the men in our city, and with all the positive things men are doing in God's house – the place was literally empty. What a statement about our society! What a statement to our young men! Statistics tell us that there are 108 million men in America over the age of 15.[6] I thought that this was a unique situation in my church, but as I began to attend Men's Day programs and services at other churches, I found it to be the norm. That catastrophe inspired my church and several other churches to come together and form the

---

[6]   Morley, Patrick, *"A Look in the Mirror – An Equipping Newsletter for Men – The State of Men in America: Foundation for the Battle for Men's Souls"*, Number 88, 2001.

Men's Ministry Coalition to support each other during events that were male-focused and in order to prevent such a spectacle from ever happening again. The Men's Ministry Coalition has evolved to include an annual men's retreat that not only unites our churches, but also incorporates the homeless population.

There is something to be said about quantity, despite popular opinion. In the fall of 1995, a phenomenon took place that exposed the desperation in the heart of men. It also showed that there is power in numbers. It was called the Million Man March on Washington. The magnitude of this event moved many of the men with passion.

It showed the attraction of bringing together a mass of men for a common purpose and it offered substantial evidence that men believe that a deeper relationship with God would possibly make them better husbands, better fathers, and better men. Most men believe that if they do not do drugs, do not intentionally violate the law, have viable employment, do not harm their neighbor, and do not abuse their families, then they are living a righteous life. That is a total fallacy.

In reality, there is nothing man can do in his own strength to achieve a righteous life. Rather, it is purely the grace of God that compels men to reach out to Him for that which can come from no other source. Each man must seek God for himself he must find his place in God.

The Million Man March encouraged men to reject the temptation of returning to their old routines after the march ended. Instead, we were challenged to continue to assemble in our own neighborhoods to help build better lives for ourselves, our families, and others in our communities.

The importance of joining forces with their houses of worship was made clear. We sometimes forget that if the fathers do not commit their lives to the faith, the son probably will not either. Unless our churches do a better job with men's ministries than we have in the past, how sad it will be that we will have let our young and old men down.

So, expect God to develop your **PASSION** for addressing the needs of the men of today. After all, if you are a man, then you were designed for greatness. The greater the passion, the greater the man. You were placed here to be fruitful, to multiply, to subdue the earth and to have dominion over everything in it. We will never live up to this divine imperative unless we take hold of it with a vengeance.

"The Kingdom of Heaven suffereth violence and the violent take it by force." (Matthew 11:12) Passion without permission will lead to problems. As a leader, no matter how passionate you are, go before the Lord to permit you to lead the men and direct your passion to ministry. Condition yourself to fast at the drop of a hat. If God has put you in charge of the ministry, your fasting has a special impact. Do not expect anyone to have the same passion that God has birthed in you. Do not force others to share your passion. Do not allow your passion to rob you of your witness. In other words, do not chastise, embarrass, or be confrontational because others do not demonstrate the same passion that you have.

PREPARATION
"PRELUDE TO A MINISTRY"

PREPARATION DEVOTIONAL
(Pray This Prayer Before You Read The Next Chapter)

O Lord, I magnify Your name
I glorify You, my Lord
I praise You
Lord, You are so good
Lord, You are so kind
Lord, I ask that You touch my heart
and touch my mind
Prepare me for the task at hand
Prepare as You will

In my efforts to please You let no harm
come to anyone
If I must yield to my brother at my expense, I will
All I do is to honor You
Make me ever ready for that which is to come

Thank You for allowing me to do Your will
I beseech You to help me do this task
in kindness and love for the building of Your Kingdom
here on earth

AMEN

PREPARATION
"PRELUDE TO A MINISTRY"

"Finally, my brethren, be strong in the Lord, and in the power of his might. Put on the whole armor of God that ye may be able to stand against the wiles of the devil. For we wrestle not against flesh and blood, but against principalities, against powers, against the rulers of the darkness of this world, against spiritual wickedness in high places. Wherefore take unto you the whole armour of God...."
Ephesians 6:10-20 (NKJV)

The idea or concept of a ministry can be spontaneous, but preparation is the key to the endurance. If a ministry is going to be successful, it must first prepare for success. Generally, what you prepare to receive is what you wind up being able to handle. A great example is the Apostle Paul. Paul obviously anticipated being attacked, so he prepared a defense that would weather the challenge until the victory became a reality. Apparently, Paul got a revelation by observing the attire of the Roman militia. Who knows it may have come to him as he was being apprehended and taken off to prison. Or maybe he observed someone attacking a Roman solider and was impressed as to how difficult it was to penetrate the full armor of the soldiers. Or maybe Paul envisioned fighting off the enemy. Whatever the case, most Christians use this passage as standard preparation for our daily lives. Most Christians realize that everything in and around this world opposes our belief. Preparation brings out a certain focus against the wicked spirits of the underworld. Preparation does not leave you vulnerable to the spirits of darkness. Always remember that anytime you take on a major endeavor for the Lord you can expect a major challenge from the enemy.

Although the "armour of God" is used as an example of preparation, there are several other effective strategies of preparation for the ministry. In II Chronicles 20, there is a story of King Jehoshaphat and the people of Judah. The bible details great multitudes of armies that included the Ammonites, the Moabites, and others from beyond the seaside of Assyria. The king called for his people to fast and the king himself sought the Lord. This is a great formula for success in ministry. Your **PREPARATION** must be based upon your personal relationship with the Lord. When God has anointed your ministry, He will also protect it, but you can NEVER think that it is your anointing or your ability. You cannot do anything without the Lord. King Jehoshaphat realized that the success of his ministry was contingent upon his relationship with the Lord.

In some cases, preparation may mean changing locations. For example, the Lord told

Abram, *"Get thee out of thy country and from thy kindred and from thy father's house, unto a land that I will shew thee."* *(Genesis 12:1 - NKJV)* This was how Abram (whom later was called Abraham) prepared to become the father of all nations. There is no standard preparation, other than seeking God first. Gideon's preparation was from the angel of the Lord. He needed a theophany to prepare this reluctant man of valor. On the other hand, Sampson's preparation was a directive administered before and after birth. He vowed not to drink strong drink, nor eat any unclean thing and no razor shall touch his head. Sampson's preparation was established before his birth. Another man whose preparation was established before birth was Jeremiah. *"Before I formed thee in the belly I knew thee; and before thou camest forth out of the womb I sanctified thee, and I ordained thee a prophet unto the nations."* *(Jeremiah 1:5)*

Take a look at King David's preparation. It was long, arduous, tedious, and dangerous. David worked for King Saul, whom God renounced and subsequently removed from office. He then anointed David as King, who became a fugitive from justice. By David allowing God to overcome his oppressors he came to know God in a very special way which made him one of the greatest biblical figures in history. David's situation should be an encouragement to those of us who will be challenged and chased by the bureaucratic systems of the church. I have observed Pastor Freddie Davis of Pilgrim Rest Baptist Church. He is a stickler about thinking ahead of the problem, which has made him very successful in many of his endeavors. Another local minister whose preparation is admirable is Pastor Eldridge Spearman of Mt. Jezreel Baptist Church. He goes over every detail no matter how large or small. They both realize the only assurance of perfection is preparation.

There is probably no worse feeling than embarking on a vision without preparation. The bible speaks of a certain Jew named Apollos of Alexandria, an eloquent speaker and very proficient in the scripture; but he was unprepared. The great married couple of the bible, Aquila and Pricilla took Apollos under their wings to expound the way of God to make him an excellent preacher.

Preparation for any endeavor is extremely important. To be prepared is to expose the vision God has given you. The bible says, ***"Then Joshua, son of Nun secretly sent two spies from Shittim, 'Go, look over the land', he said, 'especially Jericho'"***. I shutter to think how our history may have been altered had Joshua prepared ahead of time. Joshua examined the societal practices of his challenges.

The training regiment for any successful spiritual army is the ability to fast and pray at any time. Your ministry must continually practice fasting and prayer. The fasting and praying of your ministry may need to petition the Lord for another ministry in the church. When in the 20th Chapter of II Chronicles, Jehoshaphat and the people of Israel were being attacked by the multitude of their enemies, the bible says, **"And he** (meaning Jehoshaphat) **proclaimed a fast for all of Judah".** Apparently, they were trained and ready. Don't let your men wait for a church-wide fast. The bible says, **"Be ye ever ready."** (Joshua 8:4)

CHALLENGE – THE WRONG FOCUS

Humans are social by nature. Through families, religious conviction, politics, and social involvement, we identify as a society. Although both men and women are social beings, we approach society differently. We may share similarities when it comes to pleasure, friendship, athletics, business, and even romance, yet there is definitely a noticeable distinction between men's and women's style of worship and religious practices.

To view these distinctions in action, we need look no further than the men's and women's ministries within our churches. Women's ministries are typically far more

25

involved and visible than men's ministries. On the other hand, most churches find it extremely challenging to solidify the men's ministry. In fact, many local church bodies have exhausted every known strategy to strengthen their men's ministry often to no avail. Sadly, many give up on getting a firm commitment from the men in the church.

If this has been your experience, do not feel like the Lone Ranger. This is the case for most churches in America. The million-dollar question is: **How do we appeal to the men of faith?** One of the major challenges facing the 21st century Protestant community is how to bring men into the Body of Christ and keep them actively engaged.

To be sure, there are ministries like the Promise Keepers, Manpower, and the Man in the Mirror series that have made valiant attempts to capture this audience. These ministries and others have been able to motivate the male Christian population with special events or particular platforms. Still, sustaining the presence of men on any long-term basis remains a spiritual enigma.

Perhaps, we can look at Adam as the first example of the reluctant male from the Body of Christ. When Adam casually relinquished the major responsibility of the church of Eden, the stage was set for the struggle to capture the zeal of the men of faith. Unfortunately, it remains a struggle to this very day. As was the case at the Tower of Babel, today men and the church are not speaking the same language.

I believe that most church ministries that attempt to attract men fail to tap into the cognitive mentality of man's spiritual desires. They seek to soothe the male ego by just giving men positions in the church. This feeds into the male tendency to concentrate on sustaining his dominion over the earth. Like Adam, many men focus on how to improve the social, economic, environmental, and political conditions. The church, often unwittingly, feeds into this misdirected thinking; and is tentative about teaching what God speaks to the influential power of spiritual sustenance to impact these conditions.

No matter what aspect of life commands our attention, at the root is always a spiritual matter, and surely, the effective solution will be a spiritual one. Even so, many men struggle to see it that way because it requires tremendous faith. The bible says, **"We walk by faith and not by sight."** *(II Corinthians 5:7)* We have been taught to believe that if it is going to get done, we must do it ourselves. That is not faith. Faith is total reliance on God.

CHALLENGE -
THE WRONG MEASURING STICK

Throughout history, men have always assumed the roles of provider, protector, and preserver. Just look at the many battles of the Israelites, particularly their encounters with the Philistines. As you may know, the Philistines were tremendous adversaries because of their size, but they also had an incredible economic advantage. Because of the region in which they resided provided them with access to iron. Hence, the weapons of their men were made out of iron versus the bronze weapons of their enemies.

Man naturally desires to be equipped with the latest technology or the best product available to defend and maintain family, so they would do well to remember that *"the weapons of our warfare are not carnal, but mighty through God to the pulling down of strongholds."* (II Corinthians 10:4) Unfortunately, all too often, men view the spiritual approach as rather weak and passive. We would be wise to recall that King David understood how to fight his battles spiritually and he was not a passive man by any means. In fact, he was a great and fearless warrior, taking on a lion and a bear in addition to Goliath. More importantly, David was an even greater worshipper.

Men also typically rely on quantitative measures, rather than qualitative ones to judge how well they are doing. After all, men are conditioned from childhood to measure their effectiveness by keeping score. As young boys, we play games that gauge our speed, strength, and courage; we even earn merit badges for the type and quantity of knots we can tie. This tendency to measure success quantitatively continues into adulthood. We measure the size of our vehicles, the size of our paychecks, and even the size of our congregations. We must make a paradigm shift and begin to focus on quality, rather than quantity.

It may surprise you to know that, in order to start an effective men's ministry all you need initially are a few good men. Rather than quantity, you need to first focus on quality. Even so, you will never find good men until you first understand men. To establish men's ministries you must first understand ministry and then you must understand men.

The Apostle Paul instructed Timothy, **"But watch thou in all things, endure afflictions, do the work of an evangelist and make full proof of thy ministry."** (II Timothy 4:5) The Greek term for ministry is *Diakonia*. It means serviceable labor and having compassionate love toward the needy within the Christian

29

community; to advertise in a manner that would recruit a certain type of unique individual.

Men are motivated by the tangible things and lack the level of faith that women of God typically enjoy. This is not intended to be a knock against men. On the contrary, because we are responsible for the preservation of our society, we perceive there is little room for error. Thus, we have more concern for the tangible. While mastering the tangible is important, it is more important to please God. Hebrews 11:6 reminds us that, **"without faith, it is impossible to please God."**

CHALLENGE
THE WRONG SEQUENCE

The first mistake we make when attempting to develop a men's ministry is that we try to gather an army before we identify the officers to lead the army. Jesus did not select an army of men; He selected just a few good men who were able to replicate His training. In fact, they were suspect as far as their character was concerned, but they believed in the vision. Men like these are called disciples because they are able to convey the message of their leader.

Jesus knew that disciples create disciples, and although they were seemingly ordinary men, Jesus did not try to clone them. He just used the skills that they had. It is more fruitful to begin with a small group of people whose skills are transferable than to try to amass huge numbers right away. Good disciples give the best of what they have. They do not venture beyond their God-given gifts; they become the nucleus of the ministry.

Most men's ministries falter because they do not carefully select the nucleus disciples. The most significant quality a leader must possess is the ability to identify other potential leaders. I am talking about men who have integrity, commitment, vision, and most of all love for Jesus Christ. These men are not as rare as one might think, because of their integrity and humility. These men have to be sought after, they are not as vocal and visible as most men.

The best way to discover these men is to watch their personal lives. In other words, the same integrity and humility will be displayed in his treatment of his wife or his children or the other leaders of the church. Good character can only be hidden to those who lack good character themselves. The bible says, *"If the gospel (which embodies the good character of God) is hid, it is hid to those that are lost."* (II Corinthians 4:3)

THE JOURNEY

"And when He had fasted forty days and forty nights, He was afterwards hungry."
Matthew 4:2

You must prepare for ministry before you approach ministry. The fourth chapter of Matthew gives us a great illustration or a blueprint for all that ministry encompasses. Before Jesus began His ministry after the baptism of the Holy Spirit, He went on a forty-day fast. No fast is complete unless accompanied by a steady diet of prayer. Jesus set the standard for ministry and fasting and praying apparently were paramount. Jesus shows us that fasting and prayer is worship to God. It is humbling one's self for God. A leader should have a humble spirit.

The apostle Paul said, **"That you walk worthy of the vocation that you have been called to."** (Ephesians 4:1) Perhaps, he wanted us to recognize that no ministry can be effective without preparation through fasting and prayer. The discipline of fasting and prayer frees the believer for ministry. Jesus shows us that we cannot be effective in ministry unless we are free of our bondage. The apostle Paul said, **"Let us lay aside every weight and sin that would easily beset us."** (Hebrews 12:1) A ministry

32

leader must unload the weights that are detrimental to him, because the enemy will use those weights to destroy the ministry. Only, then can the Holy Spirit lead the ministry.

The weight of sin inhibits worship. Worship through fasting and praying invokes the guidance of the Holy Spirit. Any effective ministry must be led of the Holy Spirit. Only the Holy Spirit can guide you through the snares of ministry. A ministry cannot be effective without the direction of God.

Remember that it was the Spirit that led Jesus into the wilderness. When you are developing or re-establishing a ministry, you enter an uncharted territory where you must be prepared to handle the wiles of the enemy. Your spirit has got to be in tune to discern the deceptive traps that lay ahead. No ministry can begin without some challenges.

THE WORD

The Word of God is food, but it is not perishable. It is a weapon, but it does not wound. It is despised, but it does not retaliate. It is power, but it does not impose. It purifies, sanctifies, justifies, endures, and inspires. We know that God's Word is essential to the development of every believer, but you cannot beat people up with the Word. God's Word is a formidable weapon that we use to defend ourselves against the enemy and a tool to heal us. It is a turnoff to most men when a scripture comes out of your mouth every time they open themselves up. Jesus used scripture in the wilderness against the enemy, yet when He spoke to farmers, He spoke about farming. When Jesus talked to fishermen, He not only talked about fishing, but He went fishing with them. The most effective ministry starts when we first develop a rapport before we start quoting the Word. Jesus told His men's ministry, **"Behold, I send you forth as sheep in the midst of wolves. Be ye therefore wise as serpents, and harmless as doves."** *(Matthew 10:16)*

THE ASSIGNMENT

A ministry is a special assignment from God and a special assignment requires special debriefing from God. Matthew 3:17 says, **"And lo a voice from heaven saying, 'This is my beloved Son, in whom I am well pleased.'"** In other words, with that declaration, God was officially assigning Jesus to His ministry. Make sure that the Lord has assigned/designated you to lead the ministry.

When you are chosen by God to head a ministry, you will know it, because your passion for the ministry is unequivocal. No one will have the same passion that you have for the ministry.

As a matter of fact, don't expect anyone to have the same passion you have for the ministry and if you ever employ someone who has as much or more passion for the ministry than you, it may be time to reevaluate the leadership position.

THE WARFARE

Whether it is the Lone Ranger or Keanu Reeves in the Matrix, the American myth that man himself always prevails over evil. Yet, as believers we also agree that good will prevail over evil, but it's not man who prevails – it's God! When you start the ministry, get ready for a spiritual war. Just like with Jesus, once we began to envision a ministry, Satan begins to plan his counteractions. Satan's job is to interrupt ministry. He cannot stop the ministry; he can only disturb it. The first clue that your ministry will be a success is the magnitude of the attack of the enemy. *"The devil is as a roaring lion, walking about seeking whom he may devour."* (I Peter 5:8)

The greater the ministry, the bigger the attack will be. You may be attacked on your job, in your home, and even physically. Without a doubt the first attack will come from where you may least expect it – the church! Don't focus on the people that the enemy uses to attack you, continue to keep your focus on the Lord. You will eventually find that the people the enemy

35

uses to attack you don't even realize they were attacking you. It is as if they were under some sort of spell, perhaps, very much like King Saul when he attacked young David.

The bible says a spirit had taken over the mind of Saul.[7] He probably had no idea of the magnitude of what he was doing, yet, I believe God used that attack to prepare David for future encounters. The enemy wants to use you to make enemies against your ministry. The warfare is not personal it's just what manifests in a supernatural struggle.

When you begin a ministry all of a sudden, you awaken certain sects or spirits in the church. Ministries that you thought were dormant suddenly are resurrected and conflict with your ministry. You should expect that an **effective** ministry forces other ministries to move up to another level. An effective ministry will either agitate or motivate the other ministries in the church. It can be a shot in the arm to those ministries that have become stagnant or it can become a nuisance to those ministries that rebuke change. Ministry is the sounding of the trumpet to engage in spiritual warfare. It's the first punch in a fight. It's the dropping of the flag in a car race. It's the red towel in the bullfight. It's the kick-off in a football game. It's rebellion to the kingdom of the enemy. When

7   *Ibid.*

Jesus accepted His ministry, it was as if the trumpet sounded to announce the imminent and immediate war between He and Satan.

A spiritual battle will leave some scars. Just be mindful that the wounds from the spiritual battle are not physical, but psychological.

THE CARGO

God dressed Himself in flesh to fulfill His ministry. God uses the Body of Christ to transport the ministry of the Holy Spirit. God uses man's delicate body to manifest His plans upon the earth. God could work out all ministries from His seat in glory, yet God wants to give man an opportunity to minister to man.

When a vision from the Lord is implemented through man, it increases man's faith in God. It inspires the world when a divine process is carried out in these weak and fragile containers. That is why the bible is the most inspiring documentary ever presented because it captures the implementation of God's divine process.

It is important that we present and accept ministry in spite of our flesh. Jesus walked in human frame transporting divine cargo. God wants to use your human vessel to transport His divine vision. The bible says, **"We have this** *treasure in earthen vessels."* *(II Corinthians 4:7)* There is a divine package in all of us waiting to be delivered.

THE VISION

Before any ministry can succeed, there must be a vision first. God plants His visions in the spirits of men. He always gives the leader the vision first. God determines who has the passion needed to carry out the vision and implants it into that individual. If you bought or were given this book, then you are probably one of those individuals.

Habakkuk 2:2 instructs us to *"write the vision, and make it plain upon the tables, that he may run that readeth it."* Once the leader has been given the vision, he then must communicate that vision to the people of God, resulting in a "shared vision" for the ministry. It should be communicated both orally and in writing. If God has given you a vision to reach large numbers of people (and He often does) resist the temptation to focus on the numbers right away. Initially, it is not about numbers. If you are consistently obedient to God, eventually, the numbers will come.

Remember, God gave Jesus twelve key persons. He only needed a few good men. You, too, can succeed in ministry if you manage to find just a few good men.

THE MISSION

Once you have articulated the vision of your ministry, you will need to know its mission and to make it crystal clear to your team. While visions are usually lofty, far-reaching, and often grand in scale, missions are more down-to-earth, nuts and bolts, and day-to-day roadmaps for achieving the vision. Your mission will eventually blend with your passion to define the octane level that fuels your ministry. In fact, you should write out a mission statement for your ministry, just as you wrote your ministry vision statement. Every successful organization has an excellent and descriptive mission statement. It is crucial to the success of each ministry. As such, it must have clarity of purpose, so that it is easily understood by those who will help you carry out the mission.

Your mission statement can include a variety of tasks, but at its core must be the continual movement of the participants toward a deeper relationship with Christ. The object of every ministry should be to win lost souls and equip them to move to even higher levels of faith in the Lord.

Your ministry must glorify the Lord. It must taste, smell, feel, and look like Jesus Christ. This is especially true for men's ministry! Men have the tendency to turn a men's ministry

39

gathering into a business meeting. Additionally the meetings are unattractive and boring. Usually men's ministry meetings are a couple of scriptures read, a couple of songs, a couple of hymns, prayer, and then right down to business...

Because men are more comfortable dealing with facts than emotions, we think that the primary function of a ministry is to fix everything. That is, everything but ourselves. Men want to improve the quality of our physical condition, but overlook the fact that God intended for ministry to impact our spiritual condition. Make certain your mission takes this into account.

THE OBJECTIVE

Armed with an inspired vision and a clearly stated mission, you are now ready to identify objective(s) for your ministry. The main objective of ministry is examining one's spiritual condition by ministering to others. A true ministry will minister to you as you minister to others. I believe that God uses life to get us ready for eternity, yet man's natural inclination is to use life to prepare for life, which can be confusing and unfulfilling. This is why people feel incomplete. You can eventually conquer achieving things in life and still feel very empty. Life is not meant to be conquered, it is just preparation. Perhaps that is why the disciples were disappointed when Jesus told them that He would not be here long. He told them in so many words that this (meaning life) if just the beginning. He said, *"In my Father's house are many mansions, if it were not so, I would have told you. I go to prepare a place for you." (John 14:2)* The mission of Jesus' ministry was very clear. Make sure your mission is crystal clear. For example, our ministry focused on moving men into a deeper level of praise and worship.

THE TEST

There is no testimony without the test. Matthew 5:3 describes the "tempter" coming to Jesus. In ministry you will be tempted and you will need to know God's Word. Without God's Word it is easy for the voice of the enemy to confuse you. The tempter can only effectively tempt you when you become confused and desperate. In Chapter 5 of Matthew, the tempter could present ideas to Jesus that he thought Jesus might entertain. In other words, you can only be tempted by the things you think you need. God's Word says that God will supply all your needs. It does not say might and it doesn't say some, but ALL. Therefore, remember in ministry, Jesus is all you need.

THE ANGELS

Right after Jesus' encounter with the enemy, the bible says that the angels came and ministered to Jesus. When you are establishing the ministry, it will take its toll on you. You must expect this. This is why it is so important for you to be in the best spiritual condition possible. It is inevitable that you will suffer some wounds from the challenges of ministry. Although, there may be some moments of disappointments, hold on because God knows how much you can bear.

If you fast, pray, and speak the Word during your war with the enemy, God will send you some angels to minister to your wounds. Just when you have gotten so weary and you think you want to quit, God will send you an angel. That angel will inspire you to run on a little further. In fact, it's an on-going process. When you look back retrospectively, you will see a collection of angels God sent your way. Now, it may not be the individual whom you thought it would be and they may not look the way you thought; nor will they speak they way you would; and they may not smell or dress the way you think they ought, yet the Lord has sent them and you need to embrace them...

RESPECT THE FORERUNNER

Show respect for the person who attempted to start a ministry prior to you. There is always a forerunner whose research you can build upon. Because God has blessed you to take the ministry further than your predecessor you should not take away from their previous efforts. No ministry is ever unsuccessful. It takes a lot of research and experimentation to develop a ministry. You may try different things and everything will not work out as planned. You will often learn more from the shortcomings of research than you will ever learn from its achievements. All research should be considered successful. In research, you may not reach your objective, but research always meets its objective. The objective of research is to be a barometer for future endeavors. The ministry that follows you will probably and should exceed your efforts. In fact, you should prepare for the future ministry. John the Baptist had no problem preparing the way for Jesus. He told the Pharisees and the Sadducees, ***"I indeed baptize you with water unto repentance: but He that cometh after me is mightier than I."*** *(Matthew 3:11)*

Always honor the forerunner. Most great men generally have a great successor. Moses was succeeded by Joshua. Elijah was succeeded by Elisha. Saul was succeeded by David. The predecessor laid the foundation for the successors. It's important that you recognize the person who laid the groundwork. Ministry involves research, and research is merely trial and error and much can be gained from the errors. Do not discount or put down the efforts of your predecessor; all research is important. In fact, I believe that errors have much to do with how you acquire your expertise. One of the first things Jesus did in His ministry was to recognize the important work of His forerunner, John the Baptist. In Matthew, John the Baptist felt unworthy of baptizing Jesus. The Lord said to him, **"Suffer it to be so now; for thus it becometh us to fulfill all righteousness."** *(Matthew 3:15)* Jesus respected John's research!

Take time to **PREPARE** for your men's ministry, recognizing that, as Jesus prepared for His earthly ministry through fasting and prayer, so must you prepare for yours. Then you need to prepare your men. There is no need for you to have a ministry with a bunch of men on their way to hell! Bible study for men is great, but we've got to teach men to walk in their salvation. There is good reading material just for men. I highly recommend you to find specific reading materials such as *"Just A Few Good Men"* and *"Just a Few Good Men"* workbook. I suggest that you develop workshops that teach men how to walk in their salvation. Remember, ministry is always about saving souls!

Preparation also means you must have a plan. In the beginning of my attempt to bring the men of faith together, I had plans and strategies in my head. There is nothing wrong with strategies internalized, but it is hard to sell eggs to a farmer when they do not see any chickens. A good example of the effects of planning was when Rev. Frank Tucker and others wrote a detailed proposal which led to bringing together city leaders for one common goal.

Pastor Tucker, contends that *"You must show people the vision in order for them to buy into it."* Compose your plan then present to the power that can ignite the vision. The bible says, **"Write the vision, make it plain."** *(Habakkuk 2:2)* Leaders prefer to read the vision rather than hear the vision. It is only respectful to run your plan by the Head of the Church. Hopefully, he will try to sell it to the power that be. Even the great Frenchman Charles de Gaulle was heard saying, *"History does not teach fatalism...People get the history they deserve."* God deserves your best. God's plan deserves your preparation.

Case in point, in Matthew 25, Jesus uses a parable to emphasize the importance of preparation. It is interesting to me that this parable begins by stating, **"Then the Kingdom of Heaven shall be likened to ten virgins who took their lamps and went out to meet the**

45

bridegroom." Most of us are familiar with this parable. Jesus' uses these ten virgins to demonstrate the consequences for not being prepared. The parable demonstrates how five of the virgins took oil in their vessels with their lamps. The other five who were not ready to begin their destiny were caught off guard, because apparently they lacked the respect of being prepared for what God has for us. The fact that this parable is likened to or paralled with the significance of the Kingdom of Heaven is a key indicator of faith. I believe faith confirms the Lord's vision for His people.

Noah prepared for his destiny and for what appeared to be an illogical notion. Preparation will not be validated by the faithless. Satan detests Christians preparing for the blessings of God. Satan knows if he can discourage you. When you embark upon ministry, you are embarking upon a war and preparation is essential. Spiritual warfare is inevitable when you take an endeavor for the Lord. Prior to the engagement of war, the military prepares by digging a foxhole. That is preparation without manifestation.

In other words, it is like the familiar adage that *"You prepare for war in the time of peace."* You have not seen demonic activity until you have taken on a great ministry such as men's ministry. If it is one group of people that Satan

46

does not want to see unify, its men. This is why this book is critical. As I began considering publishing this book, my body was attacked. I was hospitalized three times within a few months. It was an all out attack, but Satan has no power. The way for him to get power is for God to allow him to have it.

POSITION
"ADAM, WHERE ARE YOU?"

POSITION DEVOTIONAL
(Pray This Prayer Before You Read The Next Chapter)

My God, my Master
I honor You with the fruit of my lips

My praise for You is unending
My love for You is without equal

Lord, help me to discern my position
Let your anointing cover me like the waterfall

Direct my steps my Lord
Let my heart yield when it is Your will

Let humility reign through my innermost parts
With You Lord I cannot fail
Even Your fragrance oozes victory

Protect me and send Your reputation before me
that I may be assured to do and
fulfill the assignment set before me

Bless You God

AMEN

POSITION
"ADAM, WHERE ARE YOU?"

*"And the Lord God called unto Adam,
and said unto him, 'Where art thou?'"*
Genesis 3:9

Ministry leaders should always be mindful of the value of being in the best position. During the late 60's and most of the 70's, major league baseball used a strategy that was known as the *"infield shift"*. The infield shift was designed to defend against the baseball batters who were notorious for pulling the ball to a certain side of the infield. Generally, these guys were the hard sluggers such as Boog Powell, Mike Epstein and other notable first basemen. Because the infielder got in position based on the ball player's history, they usually hit the ball right at the infielder for an easy out. Position can be a great marketing tool. That is why when politicians are running for office, it is crucial that their advertisements be in the most noticeable position.

One definition of the word "Position" read "One's place and direction relative to one's surroundings." The leader or a designated individual should be present at every significant church meeting. He may be the voice that draws support from members. Appropriate positioning is paramount to the evolution of change; it will certainly contribute to the security of the ministry. When King Jehoshaphat was lured into battle by his adversary, God placed him in the right position and the tragedy intended for him fell upon his adversary.

Men have the propensity to be drawn to large groups of men whether at church or other events than social gatherings that includes the opposite sex. One Sunday I realized the magnitude of being in position. This particular Sunday, I selfishly decided to stay home. I figured no one would miss me. After the service, I got a phone call from Minister Don Hunter who said a young man and his three children came to the church looking for me. When the young man was told I wasn't in attendance, he and his family left the church and we never saw them again. This young man was practicing Islam and I had been ministering to him and apparently, he decided to fellowship with me, but I was out of position.

The leaders of a men's ministry should go out of their way to ensure visibility. A biblical example of the importance of being in position is found in II Chronicles 18:28-29 ***"And the king of Israel and Jehoshaphat the king of Judah went up to Ramoth Gilead. And the king of Israel said to Jehoshaphat, I will disguise myself and go into battle, but you put on your robes."*** So the king of Israel disguised himself, and they went into battle. King Jehoshaphat's compromising took him out of his position. The king of Israel knew that he was the target of the opposition. So, he tricked King Jehoshaphat to exchange clothing that ultimately led to the king being surrounded by the enemy. Jehoshaphat was facing certain death. Yet, the bible says, **"So it was when the captains of the chariots saw Jehoshaphat, that they said, 'It is the king of Israel."** *(II Chronicles 18:31 – Amplified)* Therefore, they surrounded him to attack; but Jehoshaphat cried out, and the Lord helped him, and God diverted them from him.

As I discovered on the day I played hooky from church; being out of position can be very costly to your ministry. Although, it may be an arduous task, the face (or the leader) of the ministry must be in position. This may entail uniting with other ministries in the church. Chances are other ministries may be lacking a male presence. Just imagine missionaries going into hostile territory without the male presence. Youth programs without a male presence. The Pastor speaking at other churches without a male presence.

Lack of male presence in position makes the church appear vulnerable. In both Old and New Testaments, males are very dominant. However, that is not the case today. More women are in position in the church while the male makes a cameo appearance based on his convenience.

When God called me to develop men's ministries, I was astonished at the lack of actively involved men in church. It was an obvious indication that they are not in position. The words of God in the Garden of Eden rang out in my head, *"Adam, where are you?"* As I would visit from church to church, the recurring theme was *"Adam, where are you?"* I kept seeing the same group of men from each church doing all the work. The same men folding chairs were the same men working in the men's ministry. The same men singing in male choir were the same men on the men's day program. Yet, our sports stadiums and nightclubs are packed with men. In fact, some are turned away because of overcrowding. For example, you may have to wait years to become a season ticket holder.

The world is designed to appease the very flesh of man at the expense of his spirit. The flesh is and always will be very demanding. Your pursuit of fleshly desires will lead you away from your destiny. As we all know, sin has a price and most of the world doesn't mind paying it. There is a relentless venomous spirit that is in hot pursuit of every man and it is called sin. The flesh can be coerced into supporting its sinful

53

desires. It's an itch that, if scratched, becomes infected.

"ADAM, WHAT ARE YOU LOOKING FOR?"

Men seek the fellowship of other men. Yet, there are not a lot of forums where only men can come together. Men are so desperate to engage with one another that they meet at car washes, barbershops, parks, sporting events, card games, and cookouts anywhere, but church! Why is that? Perhaps, we never ask men what they want. We don't ask men what they want in the church. We just assume that we know what our men want and if they don't want what we have – we don't want them!

We have to make our churches comfortable for men to dialogue. There are supposedly 66 million men in America who do not have a relationship with Jesus Christ.[8] The average man recognizes God, but he rejects what the institution represents. Apparently, what the institution of the church represents is not appealing to men. Men view the church differently than women and seek different types of ways to foster a relationship with God.

Men communicate differently from women. For example, men do not converse via the telephone at home; and are more likely to

8   *Ibid.*

54

converse on cell phones. You have to design church activities specifically for men. Traditional settings challenge the patience of men. Where women are more attracted to the aesthetic forums, men need more thought-provoking settings. We need to present forums that make it comfortable for men to express themselves. I said comfortable – not compromised.

The church exists primarily to develop people and that cannot be compromised. If so, you defeat the purpose of the church, which is to transform lives to the glory of Jesus Christ. Once the transformation begins, the "new creature" evolves into a better husband, better employee, better citizen, and better Christian.

Men have to be approached differently about God. Men see God differently than women. The fact that God is omniscient allows all of us to see God differently. Women see God as a Savior, where men see God as Lord. Why not tailor men's ministry activities to reflect these differences?

THE COST OF LIVING

My father worked for the post office during the day and drove a taxicab during the nights and weekends. We saw very little of him during the week. On the weekends and during the evenings he rested. He maintained this hellacious pace for years and he sustained this

55

detrimental pace (with the assistance of alcohol stimulants) until his body and his mind finally gave in. This was the cost of living.

He neglected himself physically, mentally, and spiritually (thank God that during the latter part of his life he received salvation). That was the cost he paid to provide a living for his family. All this he did in order to make provisions for his seven children and a wife. He eventually moved us from the inner city housing projects to a home in the suburbs. He was the epitome of one in pursuit of the so-called "American Dream".

Despite successfully pulling us up from poverty by our bootstraps, he could not satisfy our longing for his attention. We enjoyed the benefits of his efforts, yet we selfishly wanted personal time also. Rather than voice our opinions we knew our responsibility as young men was to not put a guilt trip on Dad.

This is so typical of what our expectations are of men. We expect them to be these aggressive protectors one moment and then these nurturing providers. Life has a price, and as men we have to decide what price we are willing to pay. To live in this world will cost us something and the biggest price that we sometimes pay is our spiritual relationship with the Lord. Most men would probably say, if they had to sacrifice their souls and go to hell for their families, they would do it in a heartbeat. Are we not to make the best provision possible for our families? Of course we are! We beat up on Adam for not being who we thought he should be. We want to declare that he wasn't aggressive enough to protect Eve from the wiles of the enemy. Man will never be able to pay the cost of living because the price has already been paid. Jesus paid the cost at Calvary. He was the only one who could fulfill the debt of society. We can not afford to pay the cost of living because it is immeasurable.

THE JUDAS PRINCIPLE

We look at Judas Iscariot as the betrayer; the treasurer of the disciples; a miser and thief. We are often very critical of Judas' position with Jesus Christ, yet if we examine his thinking, we will find some similarities in how, perhaps, men think today. When Judas committed himself to the Lord, his position towards the world never changed. He thought that by following Jesus he would be a part of an institution that would impact the world politically and economically. He wanted to use his position in the church to get the world right. He wanted justice to be served to his Roman oppressors.

This is the exact same stance a lot of men take when they join church. Men want to make the world a better place instead of becoming a better person for the world. When men find out the church is not just another Section 501 (c)(3) organization, but a unique entity that changes the world by changing the people in the world through the power of the Holy Spirit, they sometimes become discouraged. We have been and are taught to change the world and not people.

We are so anxious to push men into service that we do not take the time initially to teach them what salvation, sanctification, and regeneration are all about. We don't discuss or see the spiritual oppression or that our sins (and not the ways of the world) are what keep us from being free.

Remember, ministry changes us. The world will automatically change once we change. Make sure your ministry understands that God speaks to the heart of man. We must let God change us, and we will change the world. Jesus changed the disciples and they shook up the world.

IN THE TRENCHES

One thing great leaders have in common, is they show up in the trenches. They show up on the battlefield. The great General Patton was known for showing up where his men were positioned. Not only does this type of gesture inspire men, but history tells us that it also keeps the leader focused. Case in point: when King David decided to stay away from battle, he ultimately conceived a child by Bathsheba and suffered a terrible scar on his career.

It is the same with our current leaders. The leader or the Shepherd needs to be where his men are. So many pastors appoint ministry leaders to control the ministry. Yet men want to see the general or the pastor labor with them. Men will always acknowledge the presence of the head of the church versus his substitute (no matter how adequate he might be). The pastor's presence among his men signifies a strong commitment to the cause. Men have the tendency to dialogue with the leadership and prefer to take instruction directly from the highest level of leadership.

If you want your men's ministry to be a success, the pastor must lead. He is the only one capable of defining discipleship among the men. To be sure, there are churches pastored by women, where men's ministries thrive. However, this is more the exception than the rule. The female pastor who desires to have a strong men's ministry may need a strong male assistant pastor or other senior church officials to spearhead the men's ministry. Nevertheless, the pastor's endorsement is crucial.

Men are extremely visual and are attracted to the physical presence. Pastors must be the first to demonstrate integrity, commitment, desire and love of God.

NEVER GIVE UP

Seek out pastors and leaders who have a passion for men to be restored to their rightful places in the church. We are blessed in the Washington, DC area to have Pastors and Bishops like one of the pastors I admire very much, Frank D. Tucker and several others such as, Rev. Freddie Davis, Rev. Eldridge Spearman, Bishop Alfred Owens, Rev. Daniel Mangrum, and Rev. Harold Lewis. These men are dedicated to the advancing and developing men of faith.

Men's ministries tend to succeed where there is a pastor who is unselfish and whose primary objective is kingdom building and not territorialism. Our leaders must be held accountable to make every effort to bring men back into the fold.

Then you need to gather lay leaders like Minister Cleveland Bates, Minister Wesley Smith, Trustee Michael Ingram, Deacon Gregory Wheeler, and Deacon Terry Proctor, who will unite for the cause of men in Christ coming back to the church, despite the dichotomy that church denominations often perpetuate.

A sign of great leadership is Integrity. History tells us that multi-lingual African-American actor, athlete, bass-baritone concert singer, and civil rights activist Paul Robeson once rejected an offer to play the role of a slew foot butler in a major motion picture. This enraged the producer, who exclaimed, *"Well, you won't act."* To this Robeson replied, *"I won't act then."* Robeson went on to say, *"You can curtail my mobility, but you can't limit my mentality."*

Sometimes it is necessary to hold firm despite opposition. Know that your vision will be locked in place by God and that no one will be able to steer you off course. Matthew 10:28 says, **"And fear not them which kill the body, but are not able to kill the soul."** No matter what goes down, no matter who turns against you, never give up on the vision God has birthed in you. Your experiences in your life, both good and bad, fertilize you for the impregnation of God's vision for the Body of Christ. You cure only the living because God has a vested interest in you, for only you can birth the vision God has given you, but you will not be able to manage it yourself.

Society celebrates the man who can make provisions for his family, which is basically the quality of their families' living conditions. We perpetuate a "get rich or die trying" mentality. Unfortunately, there's more dying than getting rich and if they become wealthy they choose not to be in a personal relationship with Jesus Christ. In Matthew 19:24 Jesus said, *"It is easier for a camel to go through the eye of a needle than for a rich man to enter into the Kingdom of God."*

We have to realize that not every increase is from God. Satan knows that the ego of most men can't handle prosperity without salvation. I have no statistics to support my theory, but I believe it is easier to have a personal relationship with God before you prosper, than it is to prosper and then find God.

We ignore the fact that spiritual provisions are the most important provisions. Some women unintentionally allow their men to experience damnation because confronting them would mean risking the loss of his financial contribution (especially if he makes an exceptionally large monetary contribution).

Women let men off the hook (from attending church) and thereby try to fulfill God's divine plan for the family by taking the place of the leader. It is the responsibility of the man to lead his family to their divine destination. Joshua is best known for his quote, *"as for me and my house,"* *(Joshua 24:15)* which led his family to God's edifice. Men have got to get back to being the spiritual provider. Matthew 6:30

states, **"But seek ye first the Kingdom of God and His righteousness; and all these things shall be added unto you."** In other words, put God in front of you and God will put everything you need in front of you!

Men have to get back to leading the family in prayer and fasting, bible study, and worship at home! Your men's ministry should conduct workshops and forums that instill in men the spiritual necessity to save his family from eternal damnation. Living successful public lives while leading inept spiritual lives can be very expensive.

DISCIPLESHIP

We all have a philosophical approach to life, whether we admit it or not. Everyone lives by some theory. It does not matter what moral philosophy you practice, whether it is Utilitarian, Hedonism, Existentialism, or Humanism, the bottom line is you are not your own man. If you are not living in the likeness and image of Christ, you instead are living in the likeness and image of a theory that is conducive to your worldly objectives.

The primary focus of Jesus' ministry was the training and teaching of His disciples. This is the desire God has for man. Jesus said, **"Go ye therefore and teach all nations, baptizing them in the name of the Father, and the Son,** *and of the Holy Spirit. Teaching them to observe all things whatsoever I have commanded you."* (Matthew 28:19-20)

Man has demonstrated he cannot achieve the balance needed to maintain a healthy society by his own intellect. The most effective way to accomplish this is through the discipleship of Jesus Christ. A discipleship plan gives man a proven theoretical and biblical approach to sustaining life.

We discovered a tremendous need for discipleship at our church. We took a survey and found that 7 out of 10 men in the church never volunteer their services unless asked by a committee of the church for a specific occasion. Most of our men were so conditioned to only serve for church programs, that they had no idea which ministry would allow them to exercise their spiritual gifts. Discipleship can develop men for ministry, based upon their spiritual gifts, but the foundation of discipleship is nurturing a relationship with God through praise, worship, Bible study, and prayer.

The resounding theme throughout his books is John 4:24 which tells us that, *"They that worship Him must worship Him in spirit and truth."* It is time we stop using our gender as an excuse not to worship the Lord.

The concept of men coming together to worship, praise, pray, and study the Word of God is the foundation of any ministry. Theoretically speaking, discipleship is a learned behavior. Jesus dedicated His life to discipleship. He spent years telling parables that not only established a rapport with people, but instructed them on how to live. Discipleship is relational. It begins when we develop a relationship with our heavenly Father and find out His commands for our lives. It further evolves into the development of opportunities for sharing it with others. Engaging in a relationship with Christ will make you fall in love with Him.

MEN'S PROGRAMS

Ever since I became serious about my walk with the Lord, one of the most exhilarating church experiences has been Men's Day. There is something special that happens when men in the church come together on one accord. I believe, if a man has any inclination of giving his life to the Lord, then his attending a Men's Day service will almost guarantee he will join the church. The Lord moves so powerfully in that type of event that it never fails to move even the seasoned saint to another level. If you are the leader of your men's ministry, you are probably nodding your head right now.

The church should be saturated with events for men. The church should be just as attractive to men as any sports stadium or club. Your church should have all the energy of a major shopping mall on a Saturday morning. People should drive by your church and see a thriving community instead of an abandoned fortress. Is your church the hub of the community or is it just a meeting place? Ask yourself this question: *"Why should any man want to be a part of my church?"* You may not believe this, but men really want to be part of the church community. The church has to re-invite men into the church.

Give your church a facelift by offering a variety of events for men. Ministry should not be limited. If you have a limited vision for your ministry, you will also have limited participation. Don't wait until the Men's Day Program to have events specifically for men. God is not going to wait for your Men's Day Program to send that unsaved man into your church.

Always maintain a high level of energy in your church. You never know when the Lord wants to use your ministry. Remember, a ministry should always be "prepared to minister" not become a "good ole boy" social club for the elite. Do not become discouraged because all the men in church don't jump at the opportunity to be part of the ministry. You will never get every man involved. If God did that, He would have given every man a heart for ministry.

I believe those who do not get involved may be more important to the development of the ministry than those who are involved. Try to dialogue with those who wish not to join. They represent various sects in the church. You need to know what they are thinking. You may find that you need to re-design the ministry to appeal to a mass audience. You may simply need to adjust your approach for some men. It's not what you say, but how you say it.

SANCTIFICATION

Every believer will eventually commit to living a life pleasing to God. Sanctification is the lifestyle of the Christian believer. It is the way we should live. Contrary to what many people think, it is a learned and practiced behavior. Don't let anyone confuse you by telling you the Holy Spirit will take over your life. You've got to live a certain way and then invite the Holy Spirit to guide and direct you. Your spiritual growth will come through dedication, study of the Word, living out the Word, and constant prayer to withstand the attacks of the enemy.

The directions for living a sanctified life are in the Word of God. Sanctification gives you a lifestyle that intends to separate you from sin and lead you to submission to God. Perhaps, the concept of living righteous as one can is the biggest deterrent to living for God. Most people feel they cannot live perfectly, so they ask, *"Why try at all?"* Yet, living for God or being sanctified is not about living a perfect life. It's about striving to live the best life possible and accepting the fact that you will fall short. Sanctification is of God.

Be sure to get into **POSITION** to impact the men in your church. Remember they yearn for opportunities to fellowship and need to develop a deeper relationship with Christ. They want to see the church offer something meaningful and engaging for them.

Encourage your men to attend other men's conferences. Seek out men's conferences and make this information available. Also, if it does not conflict with the church schedule, allow groups of men to attend the conference together. This sometimes moves the participants to another level of worship and inspires camaraderie. When we are new babes in Christ, the Lord pursues us, but when we mature, we've have to pursue God. You must get to the place where the presence of God can ignite your spirit.

PRESENCE
"RELIEVE EVE"

PRESENCE DEVOTIONAL
(Pray This Prayer Before You Read The Next Chapter)

We bless You Lord God
We praise You mighty one
We evoke Your presence

Move internally in us that we might come
to know You better
That we may provide a presence for all men

That your men of faith transfer our presence on earth as
it is in heaven
We beseech You to unify, your men as an army of
faithful followers

Guide us to a presence of love, peace,
and forgiveness
Teach your men how to be kind to one another

AMEN

PRESENCE
"RELIEVE EVE"

*"And the Lord God said unto the woman,
'What is this thou has done?'
and the woman said,
'the serpent beguiled me and I did eat'."*
Genesis 3:13

As the ministry develops its presence is embraced by the church. The presence of your ministry should be felt throughout the church at all times. As a young man growing up, I could feel the presence of my parents whether they were home or away. I knew how they expected me to behave. A strong presence can provide security and ensure certain standards despite its visibility. Contrary to what you may assume, there is a great disparity between position and presence. Position is more visible and Presence, in this case, emphasizes action. The world is our Garden of Eden and our presence is God's Will. Men must not limit their presence to merely the church. The community will is also considered part of the church. It may very well be that the outskirts of the church include many challenges, but nothing too hard for God.

Which is a great segue perhaps regarding the most significant presence and that is the presence of the Spirit of God. Any ministry that does not depend of God's Spirit to lead and keep

71

it is not a ministry. The Spirit of the Lord can take a ministry beyond its own expectations. The leaders of the ministry must emphasize the necessity of prayer. The more you pray and petition God, the more His Spirit falls on those who seek and ask of Him. Most ministries are created because of a lack of something or the desire for a different direction. This encourages the ministry personnel to be agents of change.

We know prayer changes things, but men sometimes have the proclivity to underestimate the power of prayer. I have seen moments when a prayer was so powerful, that it changed the atmosphere in the sanctuary. Prayer is just another form of worship. When we speak to God emphatically with hands raised towards the Father, I believe it is one of the few things that move God. The leaders of the men's ministry should encourage the men to worship through prayer. Prayer is an exercise of your faith. More than likely you are praying something that hasn't manifested at that time. The bible says, **"We walk by faith"** *(II Corinthians 5:7)*. The ministry will need to keep the faith for there will be many challenges. You can always tell how powerful the potential of the ministry has by the attack of the enemy - Big attack equals Big ministry. There are two things that Satan's strategy is set after: men and marriage. The men of faith are already missing and Christian marriages have a 50 percent chance of folding.

The presence of men is also a good witnessing tool. At First Baptist Church of Randolph Street in Washington, DC, we would have breakfast for the homeless once a month.. We would have a speaker who could deliver the Word that an unsaved person would receive. At the conclusion, we offered salvation. We presented every man with some spiritual reading material. The Gospel Rescue Ministry, led by Director Don Melvin started a very simple, yet unique practice. At the end of every breakfast, they would engage in an activity called *"Know Thy Brother."* In the activity, each man would pair up with another and they would answer the questions about each other. With this tool men got to know strangers in a matter of minutes. The bible states, **"Let him who is taught the word share in all good things with him who teaches."** *(Galatians 6:6)* Many relationships with men usually are established when we dominate each other in a sport activity. Men tend to respect each other before they bond.

No matter how advanced we become in technology men tend to use primitive behavior to establish their territory. Unfortunately, church is not the environment that appeals to the primate male. I suggest you plan fishing, golf, baseball, basketball, bowling, and tag football for the men. As they engage in each event, they get to know the character of one another. It also promotes unity. Psalms 133:1 says, **"How good**

73

and pleasant it is for brethren to dwell together in unity." Take a poll during service to inquire about what activities the men desire. Be diligent about praying together and just as diligent about playing together.

Aaron and Hur held Moses' hands up when Moses became weak. It was his presence that made the difference. The presence of men at church should be visible from afar. In other words, the temple of God is not vulnerable to the enemy. In Genesis 34:25, **three days later, while all of them were still in pain two of Jacob's sons, Simeon and Levi (Dinah's brothers) took their swords and attacked the unsuspecting city, killing every male**. Presence is essential. Satan's trick is to get you to talk yourself out of doing what God has called you to do. He wants you to leave your post. Perhaps, the most glaring example of the severity of the consequences for the lack of men's presence is Adam and Eve.

Although Eve initiated sin, Adam was held responsible for sin **("Wherefore, as by one man sin entered into the world, and death by sin; and so death passed upon all men, for that all have sinned." Romans 5:12)**. Man was the image and the prototype of Jesus Christ **("Nevertheless death reigned from Adam to Moses, even over them that had not sinned after the similitude of Adam's transgression,** *who is the figure of him that was to come."* Romans 5:14)

The disobedience of man to God's principles resulted in the loss of his position and brought imbalance in the divine plan for man and woman. This rebellious revolt (which we call sin) against God which was instigated by Satan disrupted the role God intended for man and woman. The introduction of sin brought confusion and chaos into the human experience. Hence, the challenge of men and women regarding their respective roles.

In an effort to make provisions for his family, man has left woman unattended to defend for herself. We need to relieve Eve. We have placed a tremendous burden on our women. Women continue to enter the church in significant numbers. Our women carry the church alone. That is not the role of the women. They have been standing in the gap for us, but now it is time to take our rightful place.

We left Eve alone to fend for herself in the garden. When Satan approached Eve, she was out of position. She fought a battle that required her mate's leadership. Eve was more than capable of standing in the gap, but Adam forgot to relieve her. For the garden is the example of the church. The garden, like the church, is the battleground. Contrary to popular opinion, the church is the coliseum for the battle between the enemy and the church. It is where we put on our war paint, praise, pray, and worship in warfare. We cannot leave Eve alone to fend off the enemy.

There is a shroud of silence surrounding discussion of the lack of men in the church. Even the men, who are physically present in the church, are often spiritually absent. Men devalue their relationship with God through the church. Once again, men have deserted our posts and left our women alone. To their credit, many women have emerged into leadership positions in the church. Women have made major contributions to the Body of Christ.

In I Samuel 30, we see the consequences of men leaving their post. The chapter details how King David and his men left their posts to find upon return, their wives and children had been taken into captivity and their homes ravaged. Men commit a similar offense when we send our families off to church to be at the mercy of the church. Nevertheless, many of our women have stepped up to the plate and compensated for the lack of the male presence.

We praise God for our women leaders particularly those of the past, such as Nannie Helen Burroughs, Maria Stewart, Sojourner Truth, and Jarena Lee, who paved the way for the Paula White's, Suzie Owens', Betty Peoples', Juanita Bynum Weeks' and Millicent Hunters. But there are consequences to leaving our beautiful queens behind to fend for themselves.

First of all, because of the large ratio of women to men in the church, the church has an intangible feminine distinction. Women are also greater tithers! They keep the church financially afloat and enable the ministries of the church to be sustained. The church has designed itself to accommodate the majority of its members who, in most cases, are female. Hence, the substratum of the church is female-based. The majority of men are turned off by the feminity of the church culture.

To make matters worse, in this climate, the pastor inherits the role of husband of the church, giving women directives that should be coming from their own husbands. Some men develop a disdain for the pastor (or *de facto* husband) of the church when women are influenced to make contributions both physically and monetarily. This is why a men's ministry is so important. This is why a strong masculine presence is needed. We risk the possibility of our young men embracing feminine tendencies to find acceptance in the church.

This type of culture discourages the more masculine minded young man from publicly forming an allegiance to the Body of Christ. These men become labeled as "bad boys" and some wear it proudly as a badge of honor. This, by the way, can negatively affect the young feminine members in the church who become attracted to the so-called "bad boys". Once again, a strong men's presence can be very effective at discouraging this scenario. A strong men's ministry will translate into a strong men's presence and will relieve Eve. Don't be content to allow the women in the church to do the work designed for men. Make your **PRESENCE** count rather than being a casual observer.

In a conversation with one of my mentors, Deacon Percy Baynes reminded me of the significance of the wall. We expounded on the theory that walls represent having an impact on the environment. The presence of men in the church has a great influence on the environment. When the warriors are present, the fortress (church) seems less vulnerable. We should act like season ticket holders to the church. You would not give your ticket away and miss a game. Well, take the same stance with the church. Your presence is essential. Develop a security force of men that are present at all activities.

Imagine dropping off your child at an event that leaves him or her vulnerable because there is a lack of the presence of men. Men are attracted to uniforms and giving directives that protect our women and children. It also may be an attraction to the unsaved men passing by the church. Your presence is a presentation of the new masculinity of the church.

PERSECUTION
"REBUILDING THE WALL"

PERSECUTION DEVOTIONAL
(Pray This Prayer Before You Read The Next Chapter)

O Lord we love You
Your name is sweet music to my ears

I'd like to declare that it was I
who discovered You
Yet, we know You found us and called us
Your friend

We realize that your friends must be ready
for persecution
We know that we can only endure persecution with You

Lord, if it be Your divine will
Be a strong tower
Let me feel the cool of being under the secret place
of the Most High

Lord, You are my refuse
You are my fortress

For You are El Shaddai - the All Mighty

Walk with me through the valley of
the shadow of death and I will dwell with You through
persecution forever

AMEN

PERSECUTION
"REBUILDING THE WALL"

"And they said, 'Let us rise up and build.'"
Nehemiah 2:18

One can only imagine what went through the mind of Nehemiah as he gazed upon what was formerly the wall of Jerusalem. He could only wonder of the great significance this former divine structure meant to the history of his people. Any ministry not expecting persecution is not expecting persecution is not expecting victory. Persecution gives a sense of appreciation for the value of the achievement. In 1968, after the assassination of Martin Luther King, Jr., I watched outside of my window as Washington, DC went up in flames. Some of the ruins were left for years. Now in 2007 the city is getting a major facelift. Someone envisioned the rubble and ruins as a potential gold mine.

There are those of us that detest observing what once was, which now is rubble. Anthropologists are motivated by what used to be and they envision what once was. There are stories of human life from centuries ago buried in the annals of earth that echo through the corridors of time. Walls represent an established culture whether it's the Berlin Wall or the walls of Jerusalem. Walls represent exclusion. Walls represent strength. When the walls have fallen all those attributes are lost. The fall of any great empire began with its walls and the first thing restored are the walls. As long as the walls are up, there is a chance to survive anything. It sets up a courageous endeavor. It is meant to pick up the pieces and start again. Just like a puzzle, the hard test is when you take out the first piece and it doesn't look like you will be able to connect the whole picture. When the walls of Jerusalem fell, it indicated an end of an era.

It appears that the walls have fallen again, much like with Ezra and Nehemiah. Before we deliberate on the contributions of these great men, let us ask how or why the walls came down in the first place. Perhaps we may gain some insight into today's challenge to rebuild. I want you to keep in mind only 50,000 people returned to Jerusalem with Ezra and Nehemiah. It only took a remnant or a small fraction of those who decided to leave their captivity.

The walls of Jerusalem (or Jebus, land of the Jebusites) were considered invincible. The invincibility in the minds of the people was not attributed to the power of the Lord. It may behoove you to remember, any undertaking in ministry is dependent upon the power of God. Don't seek God for restoration and then turn around and credit yourself. Joshua and his people drove out the Jebusites. King David again captured it and made it Israel's capital, where the ark of the covenant was maintained.

It came to be identified as "The City of God". The temple was constructed under the leadership of David's son, Solomon. With Jerusalem as the core city, Israel reached its zenith both politically and economically. Prophets Micah and Jeremiah cautioned the people to not deem themselves invincible, but to recognize God as the only invincible identity spiritual or physical.

In December 598 BC, God allowed the Babylonians to march on the city of Jerusalem. By March 597 (just about a year later) Jehoiakim surrendered the city to Babylonian King Nebuchadnezzar II (who history records as the great king of the Neo-Babylonian Period. In August of 587 Jerusalem was burned to the ground and the great temple was destroyed. The remaining people lay at the mercy of the preceding empires.

Eventually, the Persian Empire came into prominence and we reach the reign of King Artaxexes. Nehemiah was the king's cupbearer. During this period of history, a cupbearer was a very prominent position. It was a position of influence. In your men's ministry, you need an individual who is held in high regard by the Pastor. Everyone cannot gain the trust to get the pastor's ear. It takes years of nurturing a relationship with the pastor. You have a Nehemiah in your ministry.

84

There comes a period in the history of every church where a Nehemiah arises. Nehemiah made things happen. He made things happen, because he was anointed. There is no power that can deny a man of God who has been anointed by God. Nehemiah was such he made Ezra influence the restoration of the temple (with the aid of Haggai and Zerubbabel). Nehemiah's job was to let the world know that a vision from God has to be fortified.

Remember, these are the pastor's people and you may be like Joab, the commander and chief, but you must always respect the shepherd of the church. This also ensures the pastor's support. You never want to go over the head of the pastor. Sit down one-on-one and seek what the pastor's expectations are for his men. It is crucial for the pastor to validate ministry from the pulpit. Rebuilding challenges the authorities to be. If you have a pastor who is insecure about himself, he will feel threatened by what he does not understand. He may want to take control (or at least appear to be) and try to delegate the mission that God gave to you. I have been blessed to always receive shepherds that are supportive.

I was a very poor example earlier in the men's ministry. Someone wrote a negative e-mail filled with fallacies. I was determined to confront this person with an aggressive

85

disposition. Fortunately, Rev. Frank Tucker spoke with me and cautioned me that this type of persecution comes with the territory. You have to learn how to handle persecution. When you are leading a ministry, you become a high profile person and you will make mistakes. In Matthew 16:24 Jesus declares to His disciples, ***"If any man will come after me, let him deny himself and take up his cross and follow me."*** In this synopsis of a disciple's job description, I get the idea that Jesus is not only cautioning about potential persecution, but also how to handle the persecution. The cross is the key. You can't just grab a cross and pick it up any kind of way. You've got to handle the cross a certain way.

When President Bill Clinton found himself enduring national humiliation for his infidelity, he continued on with his duties. No one is perfect and errors will be magnified several times over. Pastor Frank Tucker cautioned me to keep my head up despite persecution. In other words, handle it!

The definition for persecution is "to harass or oppress with ill-treatment". The operative word in this definition is oppress. One synonym for oppressed is depress. You can only depress something if it has potential. So, persecution is the one of the first signs of the future success of your ministry. Your opposition may not even know why it's opposing you. Just know that you are being persecuted because you have something worth opposing. A great example is Nehemiah.

Nehemiah was one of the greatest leaders in history. Like most great leaders, he was a man of prayer and commitment to God. The purpose of ministry is to increase or enhance the spiritual lives of all involved. God doesn't assign us to ministry because He needs us and He wants to help us. I can't emphasize enough for the leadership to be obedient to God and have a strong prayer life. I say "prayer life" because it should not be a ritual, but a lifestyle.

The foundation of Nehemiah's ministry was prayer. It began with prayer and it was sustained by prayer. He and Ezra motivated a group of people to fulfill an assignment from God. God sent a group of men to approach Nehemiah to rebuild His ministry. It was a vacant ministry that God had allowed to be torn down because of disobedience. Their predecessors left them a foundation that was torn down by their opposition.

Nehemiah took with him men who were secure in their abilities. Nehemiah has the needed vision. A visionary is one who identifies what the needs are before they become a hindrance. When you are recruiting brothers, you must assure them that all they have to do is what they already do well.

IF YOU ARE OFFENDED BY THE FOLLOWING STATEMENT, IT MAY BEHOOVE YOU TO DISCONTINUE READING THIS PUBLICATION.

The main objective after you have established the foundation of the ministry and have your soldiers in the men's ministry, is to leave the church foxholes and go therefore to the highways and by-ways to compel the unsaved to the Lord. The men's ministry must draw the unsaved men to the ministry. The main purpose of the men's ministry is to minister.

A ministry is intended to serve the world a healthy serving of Jesus Christ. The Psalmist states, **"Oh taste and see that the Lord is good."** *(Psalms 34:8)* The church must act as a fortress from which the ministries of the church attack the forces of darkness in the world, and if wounded return back to the edifice. There must be healing by the gospel of Jesus the Christ through the power of the Holy Spirit. If this is not the objective of the leadership, you may be contributing to the building of a glorified society that will spend eternity in hell.

Nehemiah's ministry was reconstructed with the remnant ministry, but it was not without some Controversy, Opposition,

88

Resistance, and Encounters. So many ministries fail because they do not anticipate the C.O.R.E. principles.

Controversy

Opposition

Resistance

Encounters

Many ministries fail because they are unable to grasp the significance of the C.O.R.E. The C.O.R.E. must be embraced because it develops the character of the ministry. Without the C.O.R.E., the mission of the ministry is unclear. You can't have a successful ministry without experiencing the C.O.R.E. If you are in ministry, don't expect the enemy to sit back and cheer you on. When you do your job well, expect the opposition to make just as hard of an effort. The enemy needs to destroy just as much as you need to build.

Most ministries are resurrected projects. They have to be rebuilt from an abandoned ministry. The ministry was left unattended and the leader probably let the enemy steal his passion. It is now an incomplete frame with an old foundation. You also have to be careful with an old foundation. An old foundation has to be delicately examined. Nehemiah acted on the suggestions of the people who knew something about that particular ministry. Every ministry has its own personality and it's a good idea to confer with those who understand the culture of the ministry. This is similar to rebuilding a wall, as was the case with Nehemiah. By this, I mean the so-called new ministries attempt to begin but fall and run short of materials prior to completion.

Among the first things to be rebuilt in a ministry are the hearts of the people. Most people leave ministries because their hearts have been broken. They may have believed in the cause of a ministry only to be led astray. A ministry has to rebuild the hearts of those who have been discouraged. Don't forget, most folks in your church came from another church. Chances are they left their old church because of a disappointing experience in a ministry.

You cannot run from your ministry. You have to be careful of discouragement. Discouragement is a spirit that will try to run you out of your ministry. Discouragement in ministry can leave you with a chip on your shoulder. Everywhere you go, you will carry that chip into the next ministry. You have to learn to face the discouragement, its part of the process. Ministry in itself is not for the faint of heart. Although you will face the C.O.R.E., God will do for you what He did for David when he fought

Goliath. He will slay the enemy and use the same sword they used against you to behead the C.O.R.E.

For example, Nehemiah's ministry was challenged by Sanballat the Horonite, Tobiah the Ammonite, and Gehem the Arab. The collaborative attacks on Nehemiah actually worked in his favor. Because of the collaborative efforts of the enemy, Nehemiah formed a coalition of men and finished the project in 52 days! The C.O.R.E. can be very responsible for the success of your ministry. The enemy forces ministries into existence.

The enemy will attack your ministry, but he cannot penetrate it only you can let him in. The enemy has only one entrance into your life. He can only enter through the darkness. In other words, when you let the darkness of sin into your life, you also let the enemy into your ministry. Unfortunately, whether it is a Sampson or Solomon, many men have allowed sin to misdirect their lives. For example, Solomon was known for his wisdom but he could not defend himself against the lust demon. In I Kings 11:1-2 it states, ***"King Solomon, however, loved many foreign women besides Pharaoh's daughter, Moabites, Ammonites, Edomites, Siderites and Hittites. They were from a nation about which the Lord had told the Israelites, 'You must not intermarry with*** *them, because they will surely turn your hearts after their gods.'"*

The enemy has only one means of transportation. He can only travel through sin. He cannot enter on his own. God merely allows him to attack the ministry, but not to enter the ministry. If you let the enemy in, the bible says, he is only capable of doing three things. He will kill, steal, or destroy your ministry. He cannot love. He cannot help. He will hurt. So, don't let him in the first place. Keep sin out of your life.

PERSISTENCE
"IF YOU PUT UP, THEY WILL SHOW UP"

PERSISTENCE DEVOTIONAL
(Pray This Prayer Before You Read The Next Chapter)

Father, I worship You
I am in awe of Your aura
I glorify You

I bow down before You
Please, forgive me of my sins
Wash me that I come before You
Your grace is Your love
Your mercy is the most benevolent act ever
Thank You for allowing Your Holy Spirit
to guide me

Lord, teach me to stand
Teach me to be persistent without causing enmity
from my brother
Gird me up beyond reason
Prop me up where I am leaning

You are a triumphant God
Help me Lord, to be what you have
called me to be

I need You because I am nothing without
Your spirit
Stay near me
Let me feel your presence
I will always stand for You

AMEN

PERSISTENCE
"IF YOU PUT UP, THEY WILL SHOW UP"

*"And Moses answered and said,
'But, behold, they will not believe me,
nor hearken unto my voice: for they will say,
'The Lord hath not appeared unto thee.'"*
Exodus 21:1

Perhaps, the most critical component of establishing or salvaging any ministry is having a persistent spirit. Faithfulness and persistence share many sentiments. For example, they both must be maintained despite any visible evidence. It's like stepping out without seeing something to step on. It's like jumping out without seeing anything to jump on. It's believing when there is nothing to believe in.

Donnie McClurkin rose to stardom with his hit recording "Stand." The lyrics of the song say, *"After you've done all you can just stand."* This may well be the most difficult of all the seven strategies. To stand may sound like the easiest of all the suggestions, but to stand in the face of ridicule, rumors, you must STAND. You must stand despite the lies, when there is no support and when you are blatantly rejected. Persistence is an attribute a leader has to learn. In all your standing, you have to love those that oppose you. Your persistence will eventually pay off. Persistence in the end will become triumph!

The best example of triumph through adversity is the Cross. On a hill called Calvary (Latin for skull). The shape of the land resembled a skull. Jesus had to be persistent. He was born for the moment. He was born to right the wrong of the first Adam. With all power in his hands, He refrained from using the greatest power ever known. Jesus had to stand. Stand after being slapped and punched. He persistently stood in the face of the conspiracy by His own people. Jesus was persistent because he had a purpose and purpose is the fuel for persistence.

Persistence is having a fellowship although one or two men show up. Persistence is standing on the wall when the leadership of the church ignores you. Because Jesus was persistent, He went all the way to save mankind. Within minutes from declaring it was finished, Jesus led one of the men on the cross to salvation. Even at the cross, He stood in between sin. Jesus stood on His belief. From the sixth hour until the ninth hour, He was persistent. In probably the most grueling three hours known to man, Jesus Christ, the true light was in transition while darkness covered the land. Without the true light, darkness cannot be held off. We are all lights for the Lord. One songwriter claims, *"This little light of mine, I'm gonna let it shine"*. Even in this present age, darkness is still trying to overwhelm the light. Your ministry should be a light in darkness. If you observe some events or ministry in the church suffering, you should try to help as much as possible. If Jesus had not been persistent, the veil would have never been torn from top to bottom symbolizing that God was open to all who would come by faith.

When I implemented a men's ministry forum, I promoted it with flyers and received many verbal commitments. I stood with persistence just before the time for the meeting expired. One man showed up who desperately needed to share about his desire to divorce his wife. We discussed the problem for a few more hours. That encounter may have saved a marriage. Sometimes in ministry, you will have to encourage yourself. The Apostle Paul said, ***"Forgetting those things which are behind and reaching forward to those things which are ahead."*** *(Philippians 3:13)* Persistence and faith go together. You need faith to be persistent about a vision that God has given to you.

I know this may seem redundant, but I will continue to mention prayer. Nehemiah made prayer a priority. I will say again, that we must help our men learn how to fast and pray. When we embark on a major endeavor, you need men who can fast and pray. Fasting has to be practiced. There is nothing more powerful than a bunch of men fasting and praying. We can't afford to wait for the church to proclaim a New

Year's Fast.   To deny yourself weakens the strength of the enemy's weapons. You will never be closer to God than when you fast. Paul and Barnabas realized the value of fasting as an undertaking in ministry.   The bible states, *"while they were ministering to the Lord and fasting that the Holy Spirit said, 'set apart for me Barnabas and Saul for the work to which I have called them."* *(Acts 13:2)*

I know this may sound crazy to some of you, but I have personally fasted to the point that I saw an epiphany (that's for another book). The Apostle Paul encouraged disciples to abstain from sexual relations in marriage to lessen the power of the flesh. When you embrace ministry Satan will use your flesh against you. Nehemiah also felt that every task he took on was for the glory of God.

When you know that God has chosen you to lead the ministry you should feel like the Lord is walking with you. I am reminded of the 23rd Psalm when David claimed, *"Though I walk through the valley of the shadow of death, I will fear no evil. Thy rod and thy staff they comfort."* Perhaps, David was in the midst of his ministry when he penned this powerful and elegant message.

Like Nehemiah don't be discouraged when you observe the rubble of the wall or ministry. It will come to life in God's time. *"Don't be anxious about anything, but in everything by prayer and petition, with thanksgiving, present your request to God. And the peace of God, which transcends all understanding, with guard your hearts and your minds in Christ Jesus."* (Philippians 4:7 – NKJV) Nehemiah was also proficient in delegating. If Nehemiah attempted to handle building the wall by himself he would have drowned. In leadership you have to be careful not to burn out. If you go down chances are the ministry will be delayed. It will be delayed, but it will never be denied. If God said it will happen, it will.

When I attempted to rebuild the men's ministry at First Baptist Church of Randolph Street, I was over zealous. I became very frustrated with the lackluster spirit of the men at the church. What I failed to realize was that they were not accustomed to my leadership style. Because I was not raised up in that church very few of the men had confidence in me. Slowly but surely men began to express interest for the men's ministry. I was fortunate to have men like Greg Wheeler, Kevin Johnson, Johnnie Burton, Deacon Thaddeus Rowe, Ken Smith, Don Hunter, Raimon Nelson, Oscar Watson, and Bruce Roberson; this remnant was enough to begin rebuilding the ministry. One of the strategies I used to attract men was to let them feel the Spirit of God by going out into the streets to feed the homeless. It caught on like wildfire. It challenged the men to have a forum to do the work of the Lord. Nothing excites men more than coming to the aid of those who are less fortunate.

Men need a fulfilling ministry, for example, providing services for the less fortunate. You will find the nucleus of a ministry when you invite men to go into the homeless community. This will reveal the hearts of the men. If Nehemiah and the Lord can reach an unbelievable achievement certainly, you can develop the men's ministry that will make the church member proud to be members.

Nehemiah had to build the wall and deal with the persecution at the same time. Jesus told his disciples that they would be persecuted for following Him. The persecution may be subtle, but you will feel the sting. The interesting thing is that the persecutors don't know that they are persecuting you. They are just so vulnerable to being used by the enemy. It's almost as if they are in a trance.

Nothing frustrates those opposing your ministry like persistence. Nothing upsets the enemy more than when you make it clear that you are not giving up on this ministry no matter what. It may not discourage the negativity, but it will certainly alter their strategies. This is where the leader must discern and identify the opposition. God's leadership sometimes means, *"You may be able to stand your ground and after you have done everything to stand"*. The passage also goes on to say that **"And pray in the spirit on all occasions with all kinds of prayers and requests".** *(Ephesians 6:18)* With this in mind, be alert and always keep praying for the saints. No matter who does anything to make you give up, pray for them. A great leader prays for all – especially the saints.

Every ministry requires leadership. The leader is merely the individual to whom God has given a burning passion for the ministry. The leader may not necessarily be the most skillful or the most intelligent or the most articulate. He may not be the best to handle financial matters. He may not be the greatest communicator, he may not even have a lot of wisdom, but his passion for the ministry is unbridled.

A great leader doesn't have to out-work others. He doesn't have to out-preach others. He doesn't have to out-think others, but he does have to out-love others. Hebrews 10:25 says, **"Let us consider one another to provoke unto love and to good works."**

In the book of I Samuel 16: 6-7, God told Samuel to anoint David. God said, **"Do not look at his appearance or at the height of his**

stature, because I have rejected him; for God sees not as a man sees, for man looks at the outward appearance, but the Lord looks at the heart."

Perhaps, that is what's wrong with many of our public appointed leaders today. They have the look, but don't have the passion. Your leader may not be gifted in other areas. His passion is the only gift he really needs. Although his passion may be intense, he is likely to be apprehensive about taking the lead. Most appointed leaders are initially reluctant to assume their role, much like the great leader Moses was.

Moses was reluctant, but he had great passion. The main distinction of any leader is his passion. Remember that Moses' passion led him to slay an Egyptian who was harming one of his people. Leaders are naturally passionate people. They are wiling to sacrifice themselves for others.

God appoints you before He calls you, and He has equipped you before He appointed you. God supplied all of Moses' needs as He has done for you (which is the reason you're reading this book). You are reading the book because the desire has always been in you. You will begin to use the things that you always had.

The apostle Peter said, **"For as you know him better, He will give you, through His great power, everything you need for living a truly good life."** *(Philippians 4:18 - Amplified)* God told Moses, *"You've got it, just do it."* Moses just had to do it!.

In other words, lead by example and the people will follow. The children of Israel followed Moses' example because Moses was led of God. Even though they followed Moses (and they happened to be predominately males), they were reluctant.

Don't focus on the attitude of the people in the ministry. Focus on the direction of the ministry. The toughest job in the world is to try to control people's thoughts and opinions. The people murmured against Moses, but continued to follow God's plan.

God has given you an assignment, so just get the job done. [Don't insult God by continuing to ask Him to confirm what He's told you to do.] Can you imagine God getting frustrated? Moses frustrated God by questioning what God had ordained. Moses tried to use his speech impediment as an excuse. In Exodus 4:3, it states, **"And the anger of the Lord was kindled against Moses, and he said, 'Is not Aaron the Levite thy brother?'"** I know that he can speak well. What excuses are you using?

THE CALL

Leaders help future leaders recognize their calling or their spiritual skill level. Often times others can see us better than we can see ourselves. A great challenge for many men is to remain coachable or teachable.

To have a gift and not know where to use it can be very discouraging. There is probably nothing more frustrating that to have a gift and not know where or how to maximize the effectiveness of the gift. For example, Tim Duncan, center for the San Antonio Spurs would be very frustrated and not as effective if he were playing in the point guard position. Yet, he is effective in the correct position and a potential NBA Hall of Fame star.

Leaders encourage others to hold the position that will best maximize their potential. There is at least one man in every church who is held captive by his misconceptions. There is one man in every church who is constantly being offered a position in the church, but every year he rejects the offer. Whether it's an opportunity to be a trustee, a minister, or a deacon, he refuses to accept it.

Rejection of leadership is very common among men in the church. It is an enigma to most. It baffles the mind as to why a guy who appears to be a straight arrow will not commit.

In most cases, the individual is fearful of having to live at a higher level. He feels his life will become hypocrisy.

We all fall short and the enemy will tell you that you are a hypocrite. This perception more than most keeps men out of leadership positions. I too struggled with this concept until my pastor sat me down and explained to me that I had the wrong idea. Yes, the Lord calls leaders to live at a higher level, but not a perfect level. If you feel you are not worthy to be a leader, you are right! You are not worthy and you will never be worthy. However, you are in fact the man for the job.

Reverence of God is paramount to leadership. A good leader doesn't seek a position; he is called into the position. God does not choose leaders because they are worthy. He chooses leaders because of their passion and potential character. You are a leader for one reason and one reason only – because God called you.

THE ENDORSEMENT

Many men struggle to accept new leadership that is not appointed to them by the leader they respect. That is why the pastor must publicly endorse the leader of any ministry. Men are conditioned by society to reject leadership. As children, men are told not to be followers, but be leaders. One of the excuses men use to not join church is that they see accepting the pastor's leadership as a form of weakness.

DEVELOPING YOUR TEAM

Leaders make other leaders. It is a good practice in life to make everyone you work with feel invaluable. Leaders can be traced back to other leaders. Good leadership leads to a legacy. A classic example is former San Francisco Forty-niner head coach Bill Walsh. Due to his leadership, ten of his assistants became head coaches and four went on to win Super Bowls. Good leaders create a learning environment. Make the information that is pertinent to the ministry available to all. Every man has the capability to be a leader.

Men need a sense of accomplishment. Men are natural leaders. Your ministry should develop cell groups and assign leaders to each cell. In Exodus 18, there is a scene where Moses' father-in-law Jethro provides Moses with some very wise counsel. He suggests that Moses delegate some duties to others. In other word, he was suggesting to Moses that he begin to develop leaders.

A good leader is always trying to work himself out of a job. We see how Elijah had no problem in working himself out of a job because he was at peace with Elisha at the helm. Men are more likely to participate when given responsibility. Ephesians 4:11-12 confirms, **"And he gave some, apostles; and some, prophets; and some, evangelists; and some, pastors and teachers; for the perfecting of the saints, for the work of the ministry, for the edifying of the body of Christ."** No ministry can be single-handedly run. After Jesus defeated Satan in the wilderness, He recruited four men. He recruited men who were good at what they did and not necessarily what the ministry called for.

A true leader never battles his foes alone. The majority of David's army was so awesome that II Samuel 23 is devoted to acknowledging the great army God allowed him to assemble. A leader is only as good as those around him. David would have never accomplished as much had it not been for his surrounding cast.

Learn to utilize the gifts of the team and don't try to mold people according to your own desires. Their gifts will create room for them. Generally, your gift will evolve from a trait that has not always been an asset. For example, a gifted leader may also be one who has some control issues.

On the opposite side of every shortcoming is a gift. A person who talks too much will probably be an excellent speaker. A person who is overly curious will probably do well in security.

A person with an aggressive nature will probably make a great advocate. God can take those unpleasant traits and turn them into wonderful gifts. One of the most important components in a ministry is someone who enjoys networking and conversing with others. He is the kind of guy who can make 200 phone calls to recruit others and is not intimidated by rejection. The leader of the ministry should never handle this responsibility because when the leader is rejected the ministry is rejected. I was blessed to work with a gentleman by the name of Vernoy Hite. He was relentless in communicating a vision.

A leader of men must also show his leadership in worship. A true leader brings his passion to worship. If a leader must be an example of anything, it must be in his worship. He has to be the first to demonstrate the significance of worship. He displays the masculinity of worship before his men. In II Samuel 6, David, the warrior and leader, after bringing the Ark of God to Jerusalem, worshipped with passion never before seen or demonstrated by a leader. Despite the myth, worship is not feminine! It takes a real man to be overwhelmed tearfully by the goodness of God. If God has blessed you beyond human comprehension, I believe it is a sin to try and control or maintain your image. Never get too sophisticated to worship the Lord in public. A leader should never be afraid to be demonstrative in his worship because he can free other men to worship freely.

Allow your ministry to evolve based on the personnel and not your design. There is a difference between design and vision. Vision is ever evolving, so it embraces other concepts based on its foundation, whereas design is less receptive to change.

You must be **PERSISTENT**. Be confident that you have been called by God for this assignment. Seek an endorsement from the pastor and begin to select and develop your team. Remain steadfast and unmovable. There may be times when you schedule an activity and you don't get the attendance you anticipated. Simply focus on whoever shows up. Never publicly complain about the lack of men during the event. It makes the individual or individuals who are present feel they are not as significant as those who are absent. If no one shows up for the event, remain at your station throughout the duration of the scheduled time. Be persistent and consistent. Remember, it's not about numbers. Whatever is taking place, remember this is what God has allowed. If God wants you to minister to two or three men, you should do just that.

PERSUASION
"IN GOD, WE TRUST?"

PERSUASION DEVOTIONAL
(Pray This Prayer Before You Read The Next Chapter)

Oh My Wonderful Counselor
All of my heart belongs to You

For You have laid Your eyes upon me
Only I could not see You...

You allowed Moses to see Your back,
You restrained Your shadow from him.

Lord, we are waiting for Your return
We are preparing a holy church for
You to dwell in

We are working to remove every spot, wrinkle
and blemish from Your sanctuary

Lord, enlarge my gift of persuasion
to lead others to Your Kingdom

Allow me oh Lord the power to
persuade others of Your goodness and mercy that
they would seek You

Lord, give me a clean heart
renew the right spirit in me, so that
I will be lead by Your spirit in my endeavors

AMEN

PERSUASION
"IN GOD, WE TRUST?"

*"Trust in the Lord with all thine heart;
and lean not unto thine own understanding."*
Proverbs 3:5

COVENANT: *An oath of one party to serve
              another party in some tangible
              or intangible way that has been
              specified.*

The most flattering gesture to the ministry is when it becomes so powerful that it persuades others to accept Jesus Christ. Several covenants have been recorded between men in the bible. Abimelech and Abraham made commitments to one another. Then there was David and Jonathan; Jacob and Laban; Hosea and Assyria; and Asa and Ben Hadad. Oddly enough, man's covenants with man are contingent upon man's covenants with God. In other words, if man can't make a covenant with God, he has no chance of making a covenant with man. The bible details several covenants that God made with man (which are often called "Divine Covenants"). The first divine covenant is called the Edenic covenant. This is the covenant God made with man in the Garden of Eden. Covenants or promises call for the parties involved to trust one another.

Most of us join the church for social acceptability. We bring our unaddressed and carefully hidden issues with us. We enter the Lord's sanctuary with anxiety disorders, mood swings, personality disorders, stress disorders, attitudes and behaviors. Many of us are wounded and we join the church bleeding on everybody. Becoming a part of a ministry that will expose these wounds to the public is the last thing we want to do. We want to be in attendance regularly without committing to a spiritual forum that can show everyone who we really are inside. We want to be in the church, but not a part of it, because we don't want to get hurt again. We know that if we unite in covenant there is a great chance that we might get hurt all over again. The one thing we are desperately trying to avoid is public exposure.

When men don't trust each other, we technically don't trust God. Trust means dropping your defense. It means being vulnerable. It also means the possibility of being hurt the same way we lost our trust in the beginning. You cannot get one's trust unless you can change their persuasion. In other words, make people feel comfortable around you.

Nevertheless the question remains - Do we really trust God? One big controversy today is whether we should remove *"In God We Trust"* from the currency used here in America. What difference does it matter if we leave it on our money and it's not in our hearts. Webster's New World Dictionary of the American Language defines trust as firm belief or confidence in the honesty, integrity, reliability, justice, etc. of another person or thing; faith; reliance. The bible says, **"Trust in the Lord with all your heart,"** Proverbs 3:5). Are we capable? Can we turn our trust off and on so easily?

Very few men will admit it, but most have a big issue with trust. Our cultural expectations of men don't require trust. We don't trust each other, and in turn, don't trust God. Man's natural defense for his inability to trust is to resist or not get involved. What better way to avoid getting entangled in a situation than not getting involved in the first place?

More than likely, your ministry will have to regain the trust of the men in your church. To overcome the trust issue, a rapport must be established through commitment. Men understand their roles based upon the condition of our culture. We live in a culture that does not encourage trust.

It has been stated that a lot of our distrust stems from our early childhood disappointments. In an effort to develop trust in others and the world, we create a defense persona, which protects us from our inability to handle rejections. It also masks our fears of being loved and many other insecurities.

Man's natural instinct is to defend his family and generally, he defends them from the standpoint that he doesn't depend on the trust of others. He is taught not to trust. We practice how not to trust. In fact, you are considered naïve and immature if you trust in the integrity of society. You may even be considered altruistic, after 9/11, anthrax and killer bees; there is an apprehensive atmosphere in our society. This leads men to ask, "How can I perpetuate a lifestyle of not trusting and be a trusting person?"

Why in the world would you expect the men of your church to suddenly trust you? In fact, a lot of folks have come to church expecting to find trust, only to get hurt. Men are taught to camouflage their weaknesses. We can't afford to expose our insecurities.

Lack of trust is an indicator of hurt. The greater the lack of trust, the greater the hurt. A men's ministry must heal its wounded. A wounded army is not as effective as a healthy one. A wound cannot be healed if it is hidden. Create sessions where your men can discuss their injuries (and there must **NOT** be any women present). This makes sense when you realize that most wounds of men come from three areas. Men are often devastated as a result of negative relationships with:

1. Women
2. Other men
3. The church

I believe that most men have trust issues regarding one or more of the above. There are some men who have been hurt by all three and they subconsciously blame God for these indiscretions. One exercise to help your men regain faith is to plan excursions where men are paired together to completely depend on each other. Regaining one's trust in God is a must. Faith is the antidote for lack of trust. Men need more faith building exercises. Throughout civilization, men have a history of telling society (and for good reasons) that we should not trust men. Once men begin to trust again, then we can trust in them again.

In Hebrews 11:6, the author contends that **"But without faith it is impossible to please him; for he that cometh to God must believe that he is and that he is a rewarder of them that diligently seek him."** We must persuade men to trust in God again. If they do, they will begin to trust others. Paul says in Romans 8:38-39, **"For I am persuaded that neither death, nor life, nor angels, nor principalities, nor powers, nor things present, nor things to** *come, nor height, nor depth, nor any creature, shall be able to separate us from the love of God, which is in Christ Jesus our Lord."*

Any men's ministry that hopes to succeed must find ways to deal with this issue of trust by creating an environment where men feel safe enough to put their egos on the line.

Chances are, you will need to hone your **PERSUASIVE** abilities, knowing that men are not accustomed to trusting. Building trust may take time, but it will be well worth the effort. In fact, helping your men build trust in each other and God may be the most important facet of the ministry. Persuading hurting men that God loves them is very deep. You must encourage the men to get to know God again. Let them know that they have probably never been in a relationship with the loving Savior who gave His life in order that we can be saved. It is the leadership's job to present publications that emphasize the significance of a personal relationship with a forgiving God. If they can fall in love with God again, then they can fall in love with everyone else whom they claim to love. The hurt that most men have is so deep that only Jesus can heal. In these cases, you need to structure projects that focus on these men in the ministry. Outreach is a good way to heal. It helps men see the hurt in others and takes the focus off of them. Remember love cures all hurt and pain.

Men should also use their persuasiveness outside of the church through witnessing to others. After we secure the fortress, we must go out and let other men know that God loves them and that there is a place in the Kingdom of God for them. We become a social cult when we don't go out to bring other men into the fold. Confident men of faith should never feel threatened by new male members. Jesus mandated us to, **"Go ye therefore and teach all nations, baptizing them in the name of the Father, and of the Son, and of the Holy Ghost: Teaching them to observe all things whatsoever I have commanded you: and lo, I am with you always, even unto the end of the world."** (Matthew 28:19-20) Wow, what an awesome covenant with God!

WHAT ARE YOU WAITING FOR?

WHAT ARE YOU WAITING FOR?

If you have purchased this book or someone has purchased it for you, chances are you have a desire to see men worshipping together. You may be a pioneer establishing the ministry in your church or you have inherited the rubble of a previous ministry. Whatever the case – what are you waiting for? In the onset, you don't need anything but a vacant room and the patience of Job. Please for goodness sakes, have one meeting and begin your ministry. Don't do it the Protestant way – by having meeting, after meeting, after meeting just to have your meeting (that's a Baptist joke!). Seriously, you don't want to procrastinate when the anointing is hot. Don't project in your mind what your ministry will look like. More than likely it won't look like what you anticipated. Can you imagine how David felt? After being anointed by Samuel at the request from God, he didn't look like a king. In I Samuel 16:1 the Word states ***"Now the Lord said to Samuel, 'How long will you mourn for Saul, seeing I have rejected him from reigning over Israel? Fill you horn with oil, and go; I am sending you to Jesse the Bethlemite. For I have provided Myself a king among his sons.'"***

David began his reign serenading the king God rejected. After that, he battles the great Philistine, Goliath and before he can even bask in his moment his father has him running errands to his brothers on the battlefront. And mind you, he still has his part-time job of minding the sheep. Then he spends a great deal of his so-called reign running from Saul and eventually running from his own son, Absalom. In fact, Samuel's expectations were apparently not what he thought it was. The bible reports that "Thus Jesse made seven of his sons pass before Samuel". And Samuel said (I'm sure much to his surprise) to Jesse, *"The Lord has not chosen these."* (I Samuel 16:10) Have faith in God and don't be deceived by the appearance.

God's spirit penetrates the exterior to find the heart. When men change their hearts, they change the world. The heart is one of the things that breaks the spirit of the enemy. When you find the heart of your ministry, you will then begin to save souls. Men have the dubious distinction of combining heart and strength together. We can be like the lamb of God or the Lion of Zion. But, first we have to get our hearts right. Most men are challenged to communicate what's in their hearts. I Peter 1:22 declares we should *"love one another with a pure heart."* You may have to challenge your men by giving them a heart attack. In other words, you have to attack the hearts of men by encouraging them to communicate through the heart. Malachi contends that we need to *"turn the hearts of the father"* (Malachi 4:6). Men have got to seek God to turn their hearts. Men are so accustomed to defending their families that their hearts can be a hindrance.

The journey through ministry is an enriching and empowering one that can be elucidated. The road in ministry is an obstinate course that exposes one's mental, moral and spiritual strength. The enemy will go straight to your weaknesses. To the enemy they are like open wounds waiting to be infected. Satan wants to coerce you into the sin that brings you pleasure. We all have sins that we depend on God to arrest. The flesh is vulnerable and hedonistic. I don't care how spiritual you think you are. It's not the sin as much as it is the guilt and shame that robs you of the energy of your anointing.

When I felt that I had a calling on my life to preach the gospel, I procrastinated. I didn't quite understand why I was reluctant to move forward. Rev. Frank Tucker, who at the time was my pastor, cleared up my ordeal. He said that I had the wrong idea as to what it meant to be a minister. I waited patiently for a solution to my challenge. While waiting, I imagined in my mind several possible and familiar words or analogies of encouragement. Much to my surprise, Rev. Tucker rather candidly stated that the reason for my procrastination was I thought I would miraculously change into this altruistic individual. He noted that I must continue walking in my salvation. He told me to keep living as a Christian of integrity and character and God would do the rest. He said that God knew I would be a preacher before either one of us did. In other words, I thought I had to get myself ready for the ministry. The bible reminds us that **"Being confident of this very thing, that He which hath begun a good work in you will perform it until the day of Jesus Christ."** *(Philippians 1:6)*

We have the tendency to act as if we know what God is thinking. We think we know what is best for us. If God has ordained the ministry, He will see it through. Most of the time, our finite minds cannot comprehend what God has in store for us. I believe this is where faith comes in. When I have to trust God for something that I have yet to see. To go where no man (well, at least you) has ever gone before. I believe the more you think about starting your ministry the more you delay it. But, it will come to past. Starting your ministry may be simpler than you think. It also may not look the way you think it's supposed to look. Your ministry may begin with just you and another brother talking on the phone. It may simply begin by just gaining a rapport with one of the future nucleus' of the group. Never underestimate the power of relationships. A good rapport is a tremendous advantage. A rapport is a priceless asset. You can't buy a rapport. You can't trick someone into having rapport with you. It must come from a combination of circumstances – one may be time, another may be trust, and yet another may be an experience shared together. All with the assistance and direction of the Holy Spirit and the favor of God.

Paul, Aquila, and Priscilla had such a relationship. All three of them were tentmakers. Whenever Paul would see this anointed couple of God, they would already have work set up for him. Paul did not try to survive off of the offerings he received. Who would have thought that Paul would write Philemon, Colossians, Ephesians, and Philippians under house arrest for two years in Rome? We never know how or where God may assign his people when it comes to ministry. They key is to seek God with all your heart and trust the Lord with all your heart and lean not to your own understanding. So many people wait and wait then turn it on. Make sure that you can still be you in the ministry because a part of the ministry is your uniqueness and that only you can happen when you are secure within yourself.

The bible gives countless examples of anointed men who were constantly challenged by the enemy to keep them away from their predestined assignment. This is where a man's flesh comes in. The enemy knows that if your assignment is sponsored by God, there is no way that he can stop it. His only choice left is to trick you into destroying it. He has to trick you into separating from God. The only thing that can separate us from God is sin. The enemy knows that all of us have at least one sin that we still enjoy. The enemy's job is to get you to forget about how costly the consequences are.

Sin has made a weakling out of many a great man. Look through the history of civilization and you will find case after case of men who are remembered for their sin, rather than for their greatness. To avoid perpetuating this tragedy, we must take a stand. We must acknowledge the sin in our lives and turn to the only One who can remove it Jesus Christ.

What better opportunities to do so than to start, resurrect, or become active in a men's ministry today? I have presented in this book seven strategies to help you do just that. You now have a place to begin, a sense of what to look for, and some ideas for tailoring your ministry to the specific needs of your church.

CONCLUSION

I am ecstatic to report that these strategies led to five consecutive years of the Men's Ministry Coalition Retreats, where each year we combined 100 or more saved men with 100 or more men from shelters and treatment facilities, many of whom were unsaved. Men found this environment conducive to being very demonstrative in their worship and were so spiritually empowered that when they returned to their respective churches the following Sunday, they stood out like sore thumbs compared to the males who were not in attendance.

At these events, I was amazed at the number of men who testified to having been molested by another male they trusted during their childhood. Some threw their cigarettes away. Some committed to changing their alternative lifestyles. Prayer partners were birthed at this event. Hundreds of men gave their lives to the Lord. This was in large part due to the sacrifices of some of the great leaders and advocates for men's ministries in the Washington, DC area: Pastor Frank Tucker, Pastor Daniel Mangrum, Pastor Eldridge Spearman, Bishop Alfred Owens, Pastor Harold Lewis, Reverend Matthew Watley, Pastor Stephen Tucker, Reverend Donald Robinson, and Pastor Freddie Davis all of whom donated their spiritual gifts so those men could receive salvation.

Obviously, it will take a collective effort to restore the **passion** and **presence** of men through **persistent**, **persuasive** efforts to **prepare** them to **position** themselves to return to their rightful place in the Kingdom of God.

Lastly, if you have been called to men's ministry, remember that God has provided everything you need. So don't question your assignment run with it! Don't let anything get in your way neither distractions, nor setbacks, nor apathy. God will give you ideas, concepts, and insights to attract those you're assigned to for ministry. Don't question your ability either. With the Holy Spirit as your Guide, you have what it takes. You really do.

All you need are just a few good men.

EPILOGUE
"Why Jesus Can't Come Back Right Now?"

EPILOGUE
"Why Jesus Can't Come Back Right Now?"

"Now the dwelling of God is with men, and He will live with them. They will be His people."
Revelation 21:3

Just imagine the great multitude of the dead, small and great, who have stood strong in the faith having been saved and gone to heaven, rejoicing in God's just and righteous judgment. The great multitude all in their best linen, bright and clean and purified them and was their clothes in the blood of the Lamb. As heaven opens and a rider on a white horse appears – it is Christ with His robe dipped in the blood of His enemies while dressed in white linen the armies of heaven following Him.

Next comes the opening of the Book of Life and another book with records of the works that contains the names of the unsaved. The sea will throw out the bodies that have been buried in it. Then we see Death and Hades are ousted into the lake of fire as Jesus double checks the names in the Book of Life. When you look up you can see the Holy City of Jerusalem descending to the earth. Suddenly, there is an announcement that the Tabernacle of God is with men, and God will dwell with them (mind you, the men). While the sexually immoral, malicious savage murderers, sorcerers, idolaters, all liars and all those chosen to remain in sin are assigned to the lake of fire.

God takes away every tear from every eye. In other words, no more sorrow. Then God gazes into the crowd searching for the men and observes that 78% of His churches are women. How can Christ come back at this time? How can He come back when His men are not in position? God said He wanted a church without wrinkles and blemishes; yet, what bigger blemish can there be than an unbalanced church. Is the bride ready? I believe the answer is a resounding no! The development of men's ministry nationally is terribly significant to the men preparing for Holy Matrimony.

LEARNING TO LEAD MEN

LEARNING TO LEAD MEN

There are several unique personalities who have been called by God with the ability to lead men who are so revered that their exploits are captured in the annals of time. From Samuel the Prophet, to King Jehoshaphat to King David; from Moses to Gideon, to the Apostle Paul to Peter and on and on. These men made their mark in history by earning the respect, trust and admiration of those who followed them. Spiritual leaders are anointed by God and eventually appointed by man. Man can only see what God has already done. When God has called the leader, man first notices his calling by a desire to be of service.

The key to being a great leader is to first be a great servant. Not just a good servant, but an excellent servant. Servitude is the foundation of every great leader. Leaders need a lot of prayer, because the walk will sometimes take you through the valley of the shadow of death. Every Christian has some leadership ability – evangelism is a form of leadership. Leaders simply influence others. Whether it is through art, writing, directing, organizing, strategizing, covering, preparing, speaking, teaching, planning, communicating, problem solving, confronting, networking, listening, etc.

Leadership develops as it is engaged. Leadership evolves based upon what it is challenged by. The more encounters the more the leadership matures. Do not hide it from the bumps and bruises that come with the ministry. Each time the leadership faces an unfamiliar adversary, it become stronger. In fact, it's a blessing to endure the stumbling blocks early in the ministry, that way the leadership is ready for anything. Moses' ministry was confronted early in its relationship when he dealt with the burning bush. Before he knew it, he was challenging the great Pharaoh. I believe that when the challenges come early in your ministry, it is an indication of the powerful anointing of the ministry. The book of James 1:2 states, ***"Count it all joy, when you face divers temptations."*** It is a demon's job to stop or slow you down from your predestined victory.

Many times God will choose the unlikely to lead. One of the benefits for the leadership position is that there is no background check! It doesn't matter what kind of background you previously had. Your record is cleaned by the Blood of Jesus. When the Lord called on Gideon, he was very apprehensive. He felt that he came from such a meager background that he decided to decline, but God assured him that his background didn't matter. God wanted him to know that his background was thrown into the sea of forgetfulness. The Lord chooses us based on our current record.

The Apostle Paul said, **"Putting those things which are behind us and pressing on."** *(Philippians 3:12)* The enemy will try to use your past to make you feel unworthy of the leadership. Just remember if God has chosen you, don't let anybody else tell you different. Keep an inner circle of people with a prophetic gift. There will come a time when you will be weary in well doing. You need some serious prayer warriors. I am very blessed with my wife Sarah, my mother Edith, Vernell Queen, Ed Tellis, Kijafa Parker, and Minister Don and Denise Hunter, Rev. Walter and Denise Sadler, and Lisa Tucker as my prayer warriors.

There will also come a time when the leader stands alone. Every victory in the ministry will be connected to the leader and every mistake, every offense and every problem are also associated with the leader. The image of the ministry is a reflection of the leadership. The leadership needs the inner circle praying and fasting for the leadership. The attack from the enemy is very intense. In fact, the intensity rises according to the blessings of the ministry, for example, if the ministry is about to be blessed, expect the enemy to put up a furious attack. The leader becomes very vulnerable to this attack, because the temptation will come from the leader's favorite sin. We all have a favorite sin. It's the sin that we are weak to. The bible explains that **"No temptation has overtaken you except such as is common to man...But each one is tempted when he is drawn away by his own desires and enticed."** *(I Corinthians 10:13)* The goal of the enemy is to damage the reputation and character of the leader, therefore damaging the reputation and character of the ministry. The leader has to learn how to identify the tactics of the enemy. If something happens that's too good to be true then it probably is. If the leader has victory in their lives over sin chances are the ministry will succeed also. Good leaders only come around when God has a special assignment. Remember, prayer and fasting can prepare you for the spiritual wickedness in high places. Most of your great leaders don't want to be in the spotlight because the more that they are under the spotlight, the more that will be exposed.

A leader must be versatile. Tunnel vision is unhealthy to the leadership. Leaders adapt when it is advantageous. It is easy to overtake a leader when his movement is predictable. The leader is capable of maximizing the efforts of the ministry when he demonstrates the ability to maximize what God has given him. When Moses questioned God about his equipment to overthrow the mighty Pharaoh, God instructed him to look in his hand. There in his hand was the staff that would display the sovereign power of God. If God has called you to an assignment, then He has already equipped you. II Peter 1:3 states, *"His divine power has given everything we need for life and godliness through out knowledge of him who has called us by his own glory and goodness."* For instance, when Nehemiah and his men had to fight and build at the same time. They had to be knowledgeable in the art of war, but they were also trained in vocational craftsmanship. Whether, it was plumbing, carpentry, or designing. Because of their versatility, they were able to hold off the enemy with their weapons, yet skillfully putting the wall together. The experience of rebuilding the wall and dealing with adverse conditions. Once you undertake the leadership role, you become adept at handling the unexpected. No matter how organized you are, different challenges will come at the ministry. Just keep the Word in your hand, a prayer in your mouth and a song in your heart and depend on the Lord to get you through. Remember if God assigned you – then you can handle it. The bible says, *"God will never put more on you than you can bear."* (Ephesians 6:13)

The ultimate objective of a leader is to prepare the next leader who is of a similar mindset, but not the same mindset. A leader who has inherited his position must not be a clone of his predecessor. The people he leads must be taken to the next level. For example, Joshua took his people to the Promised Land or the next level because Moses was not allowed to. The passing of the anointing, which is the manifestation of the Holy Spirit, is a sacred procedure. As Moses did with Joshua and Elijah did with Elisha the passing of the mantle (which signifies the power and gifts of the Holy Spirit) is meant to cover, protect, and consecrate its inheritor.

Rev. Freddie Davis always says, *"That a good leader should work himself out of a job."* It is very selfish of a leader to think that he will always be in charge. The vision of the ministry must exceed the human condition of its founder. A good leader is aware of its founder. A good leader is aware of future trends and makes preparations that will allow the ministry to be flexible for the future. If you lead to the glory of God, you will never stumble over the will of man.

ABOUT THE AUTHOR

ABOUT THE AUTHOR

 Allen L. Tillman, Jr. is a God-fearing child and servant of the Risen Savior. A native Washingtonian, he attended the public schools in both the District of Columbia and Maryland. Allen is the eldest of eight children born to Allen L., Sr. and Edith M. Tillman. He is currently under the leadership of Reverend Freddie Davis at Pilgrim Rest Baptist Church.

He obtained a Master's Degree in Human Services from Lincoln University (Pennsylvania) in May 2001 and is currently matriculating at Howard University's School of Divinity.

Happily married to Sarah L. Tillman, they have served as a couple in ministry by spreading the Gospel of Jesus Christ through the Friday Night Outreach (which serves meals and witnesses to the homeless) and the Deliverance Ministry (which addresses those barriers which hinder Christian growth within the Body of Christ).

One of Minister Tillman's greatest desires is to promote and inspire men's ministries in the Washington metropolitan area. Therefore, he founded the Men's Ministry Coalition ("MMC"), which is a collaborative effort of several men's Christian organizations in the metropolitan area.

The goal of the MMC is to organize men's ministries across the nation that develop and empower men in supportive leadership through spiritual retreats and workshops. Since 1998, the MMC has held an Annual Men's Retreat in the mountains of Middletown, Maryland. This ministry has allowed over 300 men to give their lives to the Lord. The Lord has led Minister Tillman to chronicle his experiences with the development of men's ministries by authoring the book entitled "Just A Few Good Men".

He shares his talents and gifts with community and faith-based organizations. He is presently employed as the Director of Training and Employment serving disenfranchised populations in the Washington, D.C. area. Minister Tillman has promoted several "Career Fairs" that have enabled many people to secure viable employment. He is also a skilled workshop presenter. As Co-Founder, with his wife, of the Empowerment Consultant Group, he has provided life skills training for many at-risk groups.

He is a facilitator for the Church Community Partnership Against HIV/AIDS Project to educate heterosexual men regarding the prevention of HIV and AIDS. He is also an active member of the East of River Clergy Response Team.

140

Minister Tillman has also brought the ministry of Jesus Christ to inmates at the Jessup Correctional Facility. He is also responsible for bringing the gospel monthly to both those receiving in-patient treatment at the D.C. General Detoxification Center and at Father Hines Kitchen (a homeless food center).